Mastering
Pike ^{on} _{the} Fly

Mastering Pike on the Fly

Strategies and Techniques

Barry Reynolds

Foreword by Lefty Kreh

trails books

AN IMPRINT OF BOWER HOUSE

DENVER

Illustrations by Jay Snellgrove

Library of Congress Cataloging-in-Publication Data
  Reynolds, Barry.
      Mastering pike on the fly: strategies and techniques
      / by Barry Reynolds.
        p. cm.
      ISBN 1-55566-291-9
      1. Pike fishing.   2. Pike.   3. Fly   I. Title.
      SH691.PGR47   2004
      799.1'759—dc22   2003025941

10 9 8 7 6

CONTENTS

FOREWORD

Lefty Kreh

For anyone who wants to catch pike on a fly, this book is scripture. If only I could have read it in 1947 when I began chasing pike with a fly!

Some years ago Barry Reynolds introduced flyfishermen to this fascinating fish with *Pike on the Fly*, a breakthrough book. I considered it a perfect primer for anyone interested in the pursuit of pike with a fly rod. But after absorbing the information in *Mastering Pike on the Fly*, you will have obtained enough knowledge to earn the equivalent of a master's degree in fly-rodding for pike.

The pike is different, in many ways, from most fly-rod targets. This book covers in clear detail the many facets of this fascinating fish. It concentrates on the factors that will help you, as a flyfisherman, find and catch pike under almost any circumstance.

Barry clearly explains the biological and physiological makeup of the pike—what it eats, how the pike moves through the water, its life cycle, and other interesting facts. He also describes the different ways the pike locates its prey, including how pike are able to detect prey when visibility is limited and they must rely on senses other than vision, such as their acute lateral line. All of this information is invaluable to the fisherman and his or her ultimate success throughout the season.

Much of the pike angler's time is spent on lakes, and Barry gives the best scientific (but easy to understand) explanation of how lakes differ that I have seen. Additionally, he explains the complexity of a lake's ecosystem and how it affects pike location. All of this gives the angler a better understanding of how a body of water functions in terms of fishing it. If you fish lakes—even if you never intend to fish for pike in them—this information is worth the price of the book by itself!

Some anglers have been led to believe that pike reside only in lakes, and of course, nothing could be further from the truth. Some of the best pike fishing throughout the world is in rivers. But not all rivers are created equal. Barry's chapter on river pike begins with a description of the perfect pike river and goes on to cover when, where, and how to fish rivers for pike. Pay close attention to that chapter, especially the subtle differences in locating pike in rivers and the techniques to fish for them there. If you do, you will be well on your way to becoming a successful river-pike angler.

Water temperatures play a major factor in locating and catching almost all species of fish with a fly rod, and so it is with pike. Barry explains the effect of water temperatures on the pike's movements within a lake or river throughout the seasons, including the pre-spawn, the spawn, the glorious post-spawn, summer, and fall. He carefully explains when pike are most readily available to flyfishermen. Throughout these sections are helpful tips on where you might find hot spots for pike.

The tackle chapter helps you further understand equipment requirements for the pike fanatic. Among other things, this chapter shows the importance of different lines for each season and fishing condition, and that information will help ensure your ultimate success. There is also a superb chapter on the pike flies that Barry has tested over the years and that have brought him the most success. Included in this section are recipes for each of these highly productive patterns.

The heart of this book is the chapter dealing with presentations. Presentation is the key to *all* flyfishing, and Barry goes into great detail in explaining how, why, and when to use specific fly patterns. He discusses the many fly-line combinations he has used to fish each type of pattern. Barry also describes exactly how to retrieve the flies in order to provoke a response.

Many flyfishermen believe that pike only reside in distant Canadian lakes. This, of course, is not true. While North America may boast some of the finest flyfishing and largest populations of northern pike,

Barry also points out that the waters in Europe lay claim to some of the biggest pike in the world.

Pike are located over much of the northern world's watersheds, far and near, in lakes and rivers alike, and in the last chapter, Barry tells you how to prepare for a trip of a lifetime. With good planning, you can have the chance to catch a true trophy pike. His tips for the traveling flyfisherman are marvelous and offer great insight into how to prepare properly for the ultimate trip, wherever it will be.

I cannot conceive how anyone could write a better book for flyfishermen who want to catch pike on a fly.

ACKNOWLEDGMENTS

The amount of time and effort required to write a book is seldom understood except by those few directly involved—or their relatives. The countless hours of research on and off the water, the phone calls, the late nights trying to meet deadlines—all take their toll. In the end, I hope we've nurtured raw information into a readable and understandable format that allows you, the angler, to succeed. While it's impossible to recognize everyone involved, I believe it's important to thank the following people.

I would like to take this opportunity to thank my wife Susan, my daughter Christie, and my son Michael for their patience and understanding. This project has taken many hours away from my time with them, but they were willing to sacrifice to allow me to complete the book.

I would also like to thank a good friend and fellow pike enthusiast, Kevin Rogers of the Colorado Division of Wildlife, for all of his helpful biological insight and, more importantly, for his friendship. The cover art and the illustrations were provided by another good friend and outstanding artist, Jay Snellgrove. Without his talented hand, the book wouldn't have its "look."

Lefty Kreh once again kindly agreed to write the foreword. Lefty is to flyfishing what Muhammad Ali is to boxing. He's also a gentleman, a humorist, a teacher, and a man of great honor. In short, he's just the kind of person who makes our sport what it is—great!

I also owe thanks to my many friends in the flyfishing industry, including Jerry Siems of Sage Rods, Brad Befus of Ross Reels, and Marlin Rousch of Rio Lines. Special thanks also to Bruce Olsen of Umpqua Feather Merchants for providing the flies photographed in this book. No one in the industry is more important to me than Van Rollo, who believed in me and has supported me since Day One.

Last but not least, I'd like to sing the praises of my editors, Scott Roederer and his lovely wife Julie, for their efforts on this book and for helping me keep my focus, while not being shy about asking every now and then, "What the heck are you talking about?" I'd also like to thank my publisher for allowing me to write another book on my favorite subject.

There have been so many people involved, from those who encouraged to those who offered a helping hand. You are too numerous to name, but I thank all of you.

—*Barry Reynolds*
Aurora, Colorado

INTRODUCTION

The ideas in many books and articles about flyfishing work well when the water, the fish, and the weather are normal. Unfortunately, things are rarely normal when you're flyfishing for pike, and you must learn to adjust to be successful. What separates the men from the boys and the women from the girls is the ability to catch fish under the most difficult conditions. I intend to help you do that in this book.

Of course, we've all been lucky from time to time. You know what I'm talking about. You go out to a lake and catch fish like mad. You think you've learned all you need to know. But the next day you return and catch nothing!

A good angler, one who doesn't want to rely on luck, is compelled to ask why. Why is today different from yesterday? Helping you find the answer to that question is the goal of this book.

While pike are thought to be highly aggressive predators and somewhat easy to catch—and they are at times—they go through mood swings brought on by weather changes, fishing pressure, and water fluctuations. A simple cold front can move pike that were feeding actively one day to deeper water the next, where they'll seldom venture far for their next meal. This is just one of the variables that affect pike and those who fish for them. I'll describe many more of them in this book.

Every worthwhile aspect of life has a learning curve, starting in early childhood, when we're taught to walk before we run. Why should flyfishing be any different? There is much to learn at every level of the sport, whether you're a walker or a runner. After almost twenty-five years of chasing pike with a fly, I can say without reservation that every day I spend on the water I learn something new or rediscover the value of something old, sometimes with a new twist.

It's been ten years since the publication of *Pike on the Fly*, and over the course of those years, there have been many changes in flyfishing. For one thing, our equipment has improved. Advances in graphite rods and the development of specialized fly lines allow us to cover more water under more circumstances. Leader materials, from monofilament to steel tippets, have improved. All these changes have given us the opportunity to become more proficient at the sport we love.

Fly anglers have also become more educated, with books and videos on specialized topics. But as anglers become more educated, so do the fish.

Flyfishing is not always the easiest way to catch pike. Nor is it necessarily the best way to catch the most pike, although at times it can be devastatingly effective. But I can promise you, it is the most explosive, most exciting fishing you can find in freshwater! Pike have a reputation for hitting things with bad intentions, sometimes just for the pure fun of it. The rewards are great, but the knowledge you need to succeed is hard-earned.

With *Pike on the Fly*, I gave you the basics, enough information to form a foundation to build on as you became a more proficient pike angler. I intentionally stayed away from bogging you down with too many details. In all likelihood, those details wouldn't have made a lot of sense until you'd actually experienced flyfishing for pike. In writing this book, I'm assuming you've done that, that you've enjoyed it, and that you're ready to go on to the next level.

In the following pages, I intend to help you shorten the learning curve you still face if you want to catch pike on a fly rod in almost any situation. I'll describe tactics and techniques I've learned and developed over those twenty-plus years to do just that.

Basically I'm going to concentrate on what to do when conditions are less than favorable. The pike's world is constantly changing, and the fish have to adjust. So must you. After many years of trial and error (more errors than I care to admit), I've found many things that work. This book is meant to help you deal with adverse fishing conditions and just plain ol' ornery pike.

I don't claim to have all the answers, and those who tell you they do are the same ones selling get-rich scams on late-night television! I still go out each day fully expecting to learn something I didn't know the day before—that's why I fish! If you think that by reading this or any other book, you can magically skip the trial-and-error part of flyfishing, you're wrong. Nothing beats time on the water. Not even this book!

Instead, use the book as a tool to help ease those frustratingly tough fishing days. Combine it with your own experiences and develop your own techniques to suit your fishing style. I want to help you become more successful by sharing what I've learned during countless hours of pike fishing.

Mostly I want to help you get that mean cuss of a monster pike you see lurking in the weeds on your line when it seems impossible to do so.

—B.R.

ONE

THE NORTHERN PIKE

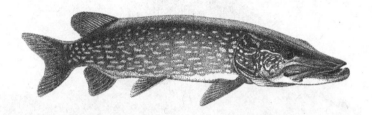

When I first began guiding anglers who wanted to catch pike on a fly, I was often asked why I flyfish for pike. My answer was a simple one, and it still holds true today. Pike hit a fly with bad intentions, and you just never know when they're going to eat it. Sometimes you can see them coming a mile away; other times they appear out of nowhere!

Pike also get big. *Very* big.

One of my most memorable pike flyfishing experiences occurred more than fifteen years ago, but it's still etched deeply in my mind and it reminds me every day why I still chase pike on the fly.

It was midafternoon, and I was on one my favorite pike lakes with two newcomers who'd never taken a pike on a fly. Low clouds and the resulting lack of light, coupled with a stiff breeze, did not permit sight fishing. Blind-casting over an old creek channel, my clients picked up several small pike, but fishing was slow, to say the least. It was one of those days when your mind starts to drift and you're not paying as much attention to what's going on around you as you should.

George (we'll change his name to protect the innocent) was retrieving his fly and started to pick it up for another cast when it happened. Twenty pounds of angry northern pike went for the fly as it left the water, launching itself into the air directly at George from a close distance. In a flash, George dropped his rod and ran toward shore. He looked as if he'd just seen the creature from the black lagoon or something worse from some other B-movie horror flick.

Pike also get big. *Very* big.

Twenty pounds of angry northern pike went for the fly as it left the water, launching itself into the air.

"What the hell was that?" he screamed.

I tried to control my laughter as I replied, "Now, *that's* what we're fishing for!".

"I don't think so," George shouted back.

After helping George retrieve his rod and regain his composure, I explained, "That's why I flyfish for pike!"

———————

Few images are more stirring than the sight of a truly large pike assaulting your fly at close quarters. But there is more to a pike than an ugly disposition and a quick burst of speed! The pike is a top-end predator that relies on many senses. Eyesight and the pike's lateral line both play important roles in how it functions and survives in everyday life, including how it hunts for food and detects danger.

To be a more successful angler, you must understand the role each of the pike's senses plays and use that knowledge in your flyfishing. For instance, in clear water the pike relies heavily on its acute eyesight, but when faced with dirty water, it becomes more dependent upon the lateral line and inner ear to locate its next meal or alert it to the presence of a predator. This versatility may help explain why pike are at the top of the food chain in their environment.

In this section, I'll discuss the life cycle of pike and explain their physiology and how they rely on and use their senses. I'll also discuss body temperatures and appetite and how they affect the pike's daily movements and moods. Throughout this section, I'll look at how the pike's inner workings and the effects of its environment relate to us as flyfishers.

Life Cycle

The spring of each year brings gravid female northern pike to shallow, heavily vegetated areas to spawn. Joined by one or two males, the larger female typically seeks out these areas shortly after the break-up of the lake's main ice. In some cases, movement to spawning areas may begin earlier, just prior to break-up.

At this point, water temperatures usually range from thirty-nine to forty-five degrees. Pike spawn in water as shallow as six inches to as deep as several feet. Carrying 8,000 to 10,000 eggs *per pound* of body weight, the mature female pike broadcasts her sticky eggs randomly over suitable bottom habitat, where they're fertilized by the male. This routine is repeated several times daily over a three- to five-day period. After they spawn, females retreat to deep water to recuperate. The smaller males remain in the shallows and begin to feed heavily.

While the number of eggs sounds high, it's necessary, since only a small percentage will survive. Many eggs are lost to predation by other fish, while others fall to the bottom and are covered by silt or other debris that suffocates them. In reservoirs, ever-fluctuating water levels may leave the eggs high and dry, when water is released early in the season to make room for the year's snow melt. Even if the eggs are lucky enough to survive, it's a tough new world for the freshly-hatched pike. The survival rate from egg to adulthood for pike is relatively low, somewhere between three and five percent.

The young hatch after about two weeks. Feeding first on microscopic organisms, they grow quickly and soon switch to an insect and fish diet. Northern pike young may grow anywhere from six to twelve inches a year for the first few years of their lives.

Typically reaching maturity somewhere between the ages of three and five, the female pike grows much larger than her male mate. While a typical large, male northern pike may be thirty to forty inches in length and weigh between eight and fifteen pounds, a mature female can exceed fifty inches in length and reach weights of over forty pounds!

The average life span of the northern pike is a matter of great debate, particularly since the very water they grow in greatly affects how fast they grow and how long they live. In general, it's thought that pike can live as long as twenty-five years, maybe more, in prime conditions.

Physiology

When a pike is all dressed up and ready for business, few fish possess a more dazzling array of tools to help them thrive in an otherwise tough environment. Known by names such as gator, snake, and slough shark, just to name a few, the northern pike's scientific name is *Esox lucius*, which sounds a bit more regal than gator or snake. *Esox* is the genus that includes pike, muskies, and pickerel. The species name, *lucius*, comes from "luce," meaning water wolf. The common name of "pike" was evidently an Anglo-Saxon creation referring to that ancient, deadly weapon.

The Latin translation, combined with the way pike hunt and attack their prey, has led to my favorite name for pike—water wolf. As the name suggests, pike often lie motionless on the bottom in the weeds, waiting to ambush prey with their canine-like teeth. Few fish stir the imagination more than the great northern pike.

Pike are graced with a splendid color scheme that allows them to almost disappear in their watery environment. Their color can even vary depending on the type of water in which they live. Typical coloration is a background ranging from dark bluish-green to almost olive, with white blotches along their sides. This color pattern allows pike to blend in very well with aquatic vegetation and dark, mucky bottoms. With dark coloration on their backs, pike are difficult to spot. I'll talk more about the art of spotting pike later.

Built long and slender, the pike's body shape offers a distinct advantage in pursuing other fish—a quick burst of speed. With its cylindrical shape and large fins, the pike moves through the water with ease and, when needed, a sprinter's speed. A pike can accelerate from a dead stop to speeds in the high teens within a distance one-and-a-half times its body length! While pike cannot hold these speeds for long, this ability does lend itself to some spectacular strikes, especially when a pike attacks your fly in shallow water at short distances! It's one reason pike are quickly becoming a favorite target among fly anglers.

Like a bad practical joke, Mother Nature threw in a healthy set of dentures to boot. Used primarily as a way to catch and hold their prey, rather than chew it, the pike's teeth are another tool that makes them more efficient at what they do—eat other fish! So important is it for flyfishermen to understand a pike's teeth that they warrant some extra discussion here.

Pike have a bottom row of extremely sharp teeth that are angled slightly rearward. In combination with the Velcro-like pad of teeth on the roof of the mouth, escape is virtually impossible once a pike has its prey in its mouth.

Pike do not chew their food like you and I do. Instead, they reposition their meal and swallow it headfirst. That trait poses a problem for

Like a bad practical joke, Mother Nature threw in a healthy set of dentures to boot.

a pike that catches a fish that's a little too big. With the teeth angled toward the rear, there's no going back once the pike starts to swallow the prey. It's not uncommon to find a pike that has choked to death on its last meal.

Several years ago, I was fishing a body of water that offered excellent fishing but was polluted with heavy chemicals buried in the ground. I often took some ribbing from friends who'd ask if I'd seen any three-eyed fish. As I was working my way toward a small slough, I noticed something floating in the water. Getting closer, I saw that it was a fish, and it had a tail at each end! I started to wonder if the ribbing from my friends was a joke after all. As it turned out, the fish was a thirty-eight-inch pike that had caught and attempted to swallow a twenty-inch largemouth bass.

Unable to expel the fish that obviously was much too large, the pike quite simply choked to death. While its angled teeth were an obvious problem, so was the fact that pike are opportunistic feeders, capable of eating large meals. Sometimes their appetite gets the best of them.

Because of those teeth, one mistake you *never* want to make is to grab a northern pike by the lower lip as you would a bass. I've seen this happen, and the result isn't pretty. A hamburger hand will bring

It's not uncommon to find a pike that has choked to death on its last meal.

your fishing day to a quick end. If you're going to fish for pike, make sure you bring your "dental tools" along. Flyfishing for pike also requires bite tippets that are resistant to cut-offs from their teeth. I'll tell you more about those things in the tackle chapter.

The teeth of northern pike have made for many great debates. Some anglers believe that pike lose all their teeth at one time and that that explains why they can become so difficult to catch. Pike do naturally lose their teeth, which then grow back, but it doesn't happen all at once, so this is nothing more than a popular myth—or an excuse.

The northern pike is physiologically superior to most fish, and few freshwater fish, if any, can challenge its reputation as the bully on the block. Next we'll take a closer look at the pike's senses, and you'll begin to appreciate how the pike has survived millions of years with very few upgrades required.

Senses

A man once asked me why a pike would take a yellow Bunny Fly.

"Food!" I responded.

"Yes, I know that, but what kind of food? Is it supposed to imitate a rat or something?"

"No, a baitfish," I said.

"Strangest looking baitfish I've ever seen!"

I could only laugh, not at the question, but at what people see compared to what fish see.

I explained to him that while fish have excellent vision, they don't see detail the same way we do. Water clarity, depth, and the resulting light penetration also affect how well fish see our presentations. Keeping this in mind, I told the man, you should usually be more concerned with the size and silhouette of your fly and how it acts in the water than you are about whether it actually looks like a natural baitfish.

Muttering under his breath that he still hadn't seen a yellow rabbit in the wild, the man scratched his head and went on his way.

Knowing how pike see your flies is critical to being able to present them properly and entice a response. In addition, by using their lateral line, pike detect high- and low-level vibrations transmitted through the water by your fly. Carefully considering how and what fish see, along with what they hear and feel, will teach you how to select productive fly patterns and how to retrieve them. In this section we'll also take a look at the pike's sense of taste and smell as they relate to flyfishermen.

By learning the basics about the pike's senses and how they use them, you can greatly increase your odds of success. In fact, only when you understand how the pike functions can you truly take the next step in your journey with pike on the fly.

Vision

The eyes of a fish are similar to our own, with a cornea, iris, lens, and retina. The rods and cones, two types of nerve cells in the retina, are also similar, with the rods processing black-and-white images and the cones color images. The higher the density of rods and cones, the better the eyesight. Scientists have found the rods and cones to be more loosely packed in fish than in humans, and it can therefore be assumed that pike, while able to see quite well, lack the ability to see great detail. This may explain why a pike mistakes a yellow Bunny Fly for a baitfish.

While pike lack the ability to grade the finer details of your recent tying experiment, they can still determine the size, shape, and color of the fly you're presenting. Since these three characteristics have the greatest importance to the fish, you should consider them the most important part of the design of your pike flies, too.

When most people think about flyfishing, they conjure up images of anglers false-casting long rods with bright lines and small, insect-like flies tied to nearly invisible tippets. This image doesn't quite work for pike flyfishermen. Pike patterns can be traced back to spinning lures, and they need to be large enough to tempt a twenty-pound fish. Still, pike flies should closely mimic—in size, shape, and color—natural food sources, just as the insect-like trout flies imitate what trout eat.

In clear waters with bright skies, you'll want flies with match-the-hatch, natural colors, such as black, gray, and white, with little or no flash. Pike have no trouble seeing flies under these conditions, and as you'll soon learn, big, experienced pike can be very finicky. Size, shape, and color are all extremely important. When the water is murky or the light is low, pike may need help finding your fly using their vision. Under these conditions, flies with bright colors and lots of flash produce well. Black is always a safe bet, since it's a natural color that can also be seen easily in poor light.

Understanding the pike's field of vision, the area the fish can see, is important to flyfishermen, too. Unlike humans and most other animals, pike have two types of field of vision. The pike's eyes are situated on the sides of the head, offering it a large field of monocular vision, 160 degrees, on either side of its body. This peripheral vision is extremely important in detecting the movement of food (baitfish) and predators (you).

While using its monocular vision, the pike's eyes work independently of each other and are highly mobile. Although a pike can see in two directions at once, it's only able to focus on one thing at a time. When it sees a possible meal or potential threat using its monocular vision, the image is no more than a shape or silhouette. The fish must decide whether to turn and investigate or turn the other direction and flee.

If the pike perceives the movement to be a baitfish or other food item, it will turn toward it and use its second type of field of vision, which provides a much clearer image. Pike have a small field of binocular vision directly in front of them, where the two separate fields of monocular

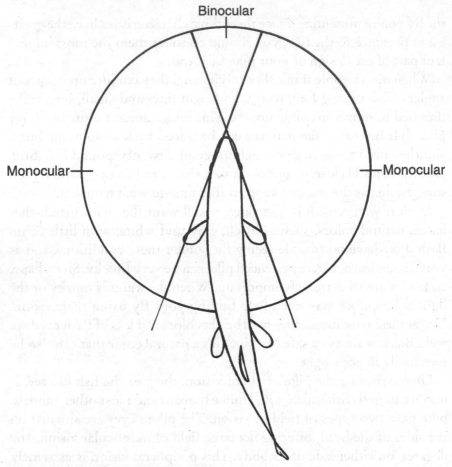

Understanding the pike's field of vision.

vision overlap. This part of the pike's vision allows depth perception and great accuracy in tracking and catching prey.

Incidentally, the blind spots you hear so many pike anglers refer to are so small they really are not a disadvantage to the fish or a great advantage to the angler. The blind spots are located at the tip of the nose and directly behind the fish. Pike typically track their prey from a distance, and the blind spot in the front of the fish rarely becomes a factor in the outcome of the chase.

For the angler, a stealthy approach from the rear, using the blind spot there, is preferred, but it's still no guarantee you won't be noticed. If

The pike's eyes work independently of each other and are highly mobile.

the pike detects you, chances are it will hear or feel you using other senses and spook before it actually sees you. Still, an approach from the rear offers the best chance of sneaking up on a fish.

I use my understanding of the pike's vision-based behavior all the time while I'm fishing. For instance, I prefer to present my fly at an angle to the fish, as opposed to a straight-on shot, thus making use of their extraordinary side vision to attract them. In addition, I'll start by placing my fly about ten feet away from the fish and gradually work it closer until the pike sees it. This allows the pike to detect the fly more naturally as it moves into its field of vision.

The fly is first seen as movement in the pike's peripheral vision. The pike then quickly turns so that the fly is in its binocular field of vision, which measures approximately thirty degrees. That's when it decides whether the fly is worth eating. The actual width of the pike's binocular vision changes with distance, of course. The farther away, the wider the field of binocular vision becomes.

By the way, flies thrown directly on top of a pike usually result in startling the fish into a mad dash for deeper, more secure water. The bottom line is, it's not natural for food to fall from the sky right into the lap of a hungry pike! Remember to think like a fish and make your presentations as realistic as possible. The end result will be more hook-ups.

Pike also have good overhead vision, but this time the depth of the water determines how wide this zone will be. In shallow water, three feet or less, this overhead view will be fairly narrow, less than a foot. In deeper water the overhead view widens. This information will be important to you as we discuss in detail specific presentations and techniques later in the book.

So what does all this mean? Knowing how and what the fish sees helps you present your fly more naturally without spooking it. While eyesight is very important, particularly in clear water, it's only one of several ways that northern pike locate their prey. Actually, pike can survive quite well without their eyesight, because they possess other senses that allow them to hunt without the use of their eyes!

Flies like the Dahlberg Diver appeal to the many senses of the pike. This fly works not only on visual appeal but also on the fish's ability to detect the water displacement the fly creates as it's retrieved. This movement triggers responses from a tool that all fish possess but too few anglers actually understand, the lateral line.

Lateral Line

When you flyfish for northern pike, you'll find water clarity that ranges from water clear enough you can see the bottom of the lake in twenty feet of water, to water so discolored you can't see your fly until you pull it out of the water. Some of my favorite Alaskan pike water is so dirty that visibility might be four inches on a good day. So, how can you still catch fish in that kind of water using flies? Certainly a pike can't see a fly in water that dirty.

In conjunction with their keen eyesight, pike use another sense, a sense so highly perfected that scientists are developing a mechanical version of it that will allow submersible craft to navigate when the people inside can't see where they're going and without the use of detectable sonar.

So what is this mystery sense? The lateral line.

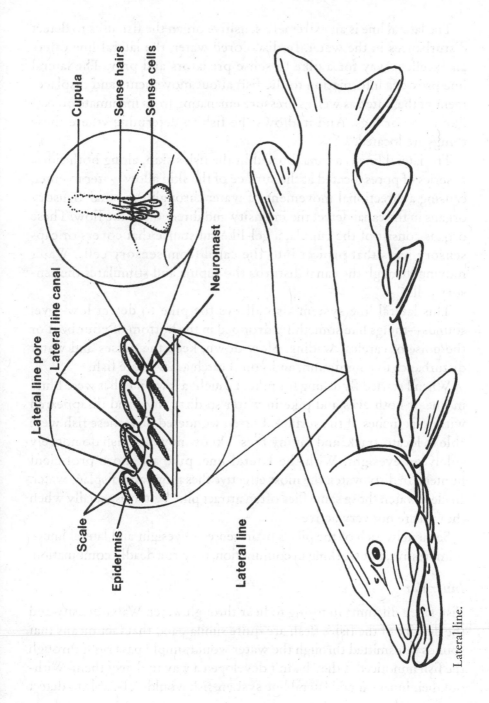

Lateral line.

The lateral line is an extremely sensitive organ the fish uses to detect disturbances in the water. In discolored water, the lateral line offers an excellent way for a pike to sense predators and prey. The lateral line provides information to the fish about movements and displacement of the water, as well as pressure emanating from inanimate objects like rocks or logs. And it allows the fish to determine where these things are located.

The lateral line is a canal buried in the fish's skin, along both sides. A series of pores located at the surface of the skin allow water to enter, causing a directional movement of water through the canal. Sensory organs in the canal detect the intensity and direction of the flow. These organs consist of the cupula, a gel-like substance that covers or caps sensory hairs that project into the canal from sensory cells. Water moving through the canal disturbs the cupula and stimulates the sensory cells.

This lateral line system also allows the pike to detect low-level sounds—things like something dropped in the bottom of your boat or the noise of careless wading. Slow down, keep the noises and water disturbance to a minimum, and you'll catch a few more fish.

When I started flyfishing for pike, I caught a few pike that were blind in one or both eyes and pike in water so dirty my hand disappeared within six inches of the surface. I often wondered how these fish were able to locate, track, and eat my flies. I know now that fish do not rely solely on eyesight. With the lateral line, pike are more proficient hunters. In dirty water, the most effective flies move and displace water. In clear water, those same flies often attract pike better, especially when the fish are not very active.

Separately, each of the pike's main senses—eyesight and lateral line—is impressive, but working in conjunction, they're a deadly combination.

Inner Ear

Fish face a dilemma in trying to hear through water. Water density and the density of the fish's flesh are quite similar, and that fact means that sounds transmitted through the water would simply pass right through the fish unnoticed if they hadn't developed a way to detect them. Without their inner ear and lateral line system, fish wouldn't be able to detect sounds or the direction of their source at all, making everyday survival tough, to say the least.

The pike's inner ear system allows them to detect low-frequency sound vibrations transmitted through the water. The inner ear's other purpose is to work in conjunction with the air bladder to maintain balance and spacial orientation. Located within the pike's skull, the inner ear is made up of bony structure that is denser than water and is thus disturbed by sound waves as they pass through the fish's body. These inner ears have chambers lined with tiny sensory hair cells and ear stones called otoliths. As vibrations pass through the inner ear, they cause movement of the otoliths, which in turn deflect the hair cells. Auditory nerves then "notify" the fish of the sounds. An interesting fact about otoliths is that they show growth rings in much the same manner as a tree trunk, and biologists can use these to determine a fish's age and growth rate during scientific studies.

While able to detect sound waves, the inner ear alone is unable to determine the direction of a noise or the distance to its source. The fish integrates information from the lateral line to determine those factors. These sensory organs work in conjunction to help locate prey and to protect the fish from predators. The next time you're clumsily wading along or clanking the bottom of your boat, and you wonder if fish in the vicinity can hear you, the answer is a resounding yes!

Sense of Smell

Fish do have a sense of smell. Although we generally rely on the pike's ability to see or hear our fly, there are some things worth noting about its sense of smell. Fish have two nostrils and odors in the water are detected by the olfactory nerves. Fish are thought to have a sense of smell that's about 100 times more sensitive than our own. Fish such as salmon use this acute sense of smell to return to the same waters in which they were born in order to spawn.

Northern pike use their sense of smell to detect pheromones, scents in the water that are released by fleeing prey. They may use their sense of smell to detect predators such as fishermen. Simply rinsing your hands in the water can alert them to your presence. This is especially important to remember when you've had contact with things like gasoline, insect repellent, sunscreen, and tobacco. These items, in particular, seem to offend fish and signal that something's not right in the neighborhood.

On a recent pike outing, the importance of understanding their sensitivity to odors became quite apparent. Two anglers fished side by side, using the exact same setup all the way down to the fly. One angler continually hooked fish while the other angler never got a sniff, so to speak. I watched their retrieves, their casts, everything! There were some subtle differences, but nothing that would cause one angler to have a distinct advantage over the other.

While I watched, the unlucky angler paused to ponder a moment. He took a wad of chewing tobacco out of his mouth and put a new one in. No big deal. What he did next, however, offered a clue to what was going on. Without washing off his hands, he immediately handled his fly, inadvertently transferring tobacco to his fly. I went over and switched his fly out, explaining that fish do not like the smell of tobacco. Laughing at me like it was some kind of joke, he made a cast and was instantly rewarded with a bone-jarring strike.

Sense of Taste

Taste buds in fish are located on the tongue, roof of the mouth, and lip. In addition, fish also have taste buds on the gill arches and in the gill cavity. The pike's sense of taste, however, has little impact on fly-fishing for them.

While fishing the clear lakes of Canada, I've been able to observe pike and their reactions as they take the fly. What I've concluded is that pike either like the taste of flies or they have a poor sense of taste. I allowed several pike to take a fly but didn't set the hook; the pike would rarely spit out the fly. The only thing I caution is that you wash your hands (not in the water you're fishing), if you've handled gasoline, insect repellent, sunscreen, or tobacco. Not only will the smell turn off the fish, but those things taste really bad.

Appetite

The pike's greatest vulnerability is probably its appetite. Pike are gluttons. A pike is capable of eating something roughly one-third its own size. But large meals may not always be available, forcing pike to feed on smaller prey. For example, in some of our most prolific Alaskan waters, pike utilize a variety of food sources during the year. In spring they feed on whitefish and small sheefish. As summer progresses, their diet switches to migrating salmon smolt. While salmon smolt hardly represent a sizable meal in individual servings, they do offer a high-protein feast when consumed in numbers.

Like all fish, pike follow a biological rule known as "rate of return." A pike must obtain as least as much energy from the food it eats as it uses in catching that food. When smaller prey is present in low numbers, pike are reluctant to expend large amounts of energy to catch them, since they receive little in return. Some anglers see this as laziness, but it's simply conservation of energy. A small meal must be easy to catch, or the pike will simply wait for a greater rate of return.

I've seen this behavior many times. When throwing smaller patterns to what I considered to be finicky pike, I've noticed that if the fly is presented close to the fish, the pike readily attack it. If the presentation is farther away, the pike fail to react. Although I expect this behavior in spring when cold water slows pike down, it also happens in prime time with optimum water temperatures, if prey fish aren't abundant.

Increasing the size of the fly generally makes the pike more willing to move a greater distance. I've also seen this work in reverse, when abundant smaller prey is on the menu and easy to catch. Under those circumstances, pike seem unwilling to expend the energy to chase a bigger target that might require more effort to catch. Downsizing the fly is all that is needed to trigger a response.

By being aware of the pike's appetite and the rate-of-return rule, you can certainly increase your catch rates. By knowing what prey is available, when it's available, and in what quantities, you can also improve your odds of success. It's really not that different from trout fishing when trout key to a specific insect hatch. If you throw a stonefly pattern when mayflies are on the water, your chances for success are slim to none.

The pike's body temperature also plays a part in its appetite. In coldwater conditions, the pike's metabolic rate slows, and the time it takes to digest its last meal increases, reducing its appetite. Water temperature is one more thing we must consider in our pursuit of pike.

Water Temperature

Because pike are cold-blooded creatures, their body temperatures are dependent on the water that surrounds them. That fact directly affects their metabolism, as I've said, but all activities, such as feeding and the urge to spawn, are directly related to water temperature. Water temperatures also affect the amount of oxygen available in the water, and that also dictates how active pike will be and where they will be in a lake or river. Water temperature may sound relatively simple, but it's a complex factor in the lives of pike.

Freshwater fish are divided into three categories: coldwater, coolwater, and warmwater. Pike are listed as a coolwater species, preferring water temperatures between fifty and seventy degrees.

A pike's temperature preference seems to vary with the size of the individual fish, so you must consider this factor, too. While smaller pike do well in colder water, for instance, they also remain quite active when water temperatures exceed the seventy-degree range, even for prolonged periods of time. The largest pike—the ones we're interested in catching—seem to be most active when water temperatures are in the fifty- to sixty-degree range.

This may help explain why some Canadian lakes that rarely see water temperatures much above sixty degrees produce good numbers of trophy pike (provided they have the habitat and food sources to match), while the southernmost areas of the pike's range rarely produce numbers of big pike.

During the spring months, water temperatures can be a driving force in where pike of different sizes will be located, when they'll be there, and how long they'll stay. During the midmorning hours, smaller pike arrive in the shallows first. Their bodies warm more quickly than their larger counterpart's. Larger fish normally show up later in the day. This explains why the pike you come across when you first arrive at your favorite pike flat are usually small fish. As the day progresses, more and more fish, including the big ones, show up after the shallows have had a chance to warm thoroughly.

Anglers often assume that since they found pike in the shallows one afternoon, the fish will be there the next morning. If it were only that simple! The fact is that movements in and out of the shallows are based

More and more fish, including the big ones, show up after the shallows have had a chance to warm thoroughly.

on water temperatures, which change overnight, and other factors, including food availability. We just can't make such broad assumptions.

After observing these movement patterns several times, you will begin to have an appreciation of the importance of water temperature. I'll go into more detail on water temperatures in the next chapter. Another thing you may notice are distinct differences in the moods of pike and how they change throughout the course of a day. While mid-mornings and early afternoons may find pike glued tight to the bottom and lethargic, you may find the same fish aggressively on the prowl in the late afternoon hours.

The Pike's Moods

Contrary to popular belief, pike are not always aggressive nor do they constantly eat. Weather, water temperatures, and available oxygen levels can greatly affect the pike's "mood." If you fish for pike long enough, you'll see them exhibit three distinct moods or activity levels. Understanding these moods will help you decide which presentation to use to trigger a strike. Throughout the book, you'll find that I refer to the pike's mood when discussing presentations and the effects of weather and water temperature.

The three basic moods include positive (active), neutral (middling), and negative (inactive). When pike exhibit a positive mood, the fish are active and can be quite easy to catch. Due to their aggressive nature, active fish can be easily provoked into striking your fly.

Positive or active pike are normally close to the surface or in relatively shallow water; they are more willing to leave structure and cover to hunt in open water than are neutral or negative pike. Pike are likely to be in a positive mood when conditions are ideal, such as the glorious post-spawn period and other times of the year when water temperatures, oxygen levels, and an abundance of prey present perfect conditions.

Neutral pike are fish that aren't aggressive but haven't shut down either. They can be provoked to strike. Water temperatures that are too cold or too warm are the primary causes for this mood. Another time you're likely to find pike in neutral is when they're resting with a full belly, waiting for their last meal to digest.

Many times these fish will lazily follow your fly from a safe distance only to raise your expectations and then slowly disappear into the depths. At this point you'll wonder who is trying to provoke whom. Neutral pike often hold in shallow water, soaking up the sun's heat (in the spring) to raise their body temperature, or they stay tight to structure or cover. With neutral pike, you need to play upon the pike's built-in reflex actions. Think of getting a kitten to pounce on a ball of yarn. I'll talk more about this in the presentation chapter.

Negative pike are fish that have shut down for reasons usually directly related to their environment. Their behavior may appear to be neutral, but their reactions to your fly cannot be mistaken. Negative fish are usually found holding tight to the bottom or to structure and are very reluctant to leave it. They refuse to budge and will not follow your offerings.

I have a simple rule when I find pike in negative moods—I go fish for something else. If no option is available to you, pay close attention to the presentation chapter for some tactics that can save the day.

While you can easily catch pike when prime conditions exist, the ability to catch pike during the "other" times will separate weekend pike anglers from the pike slayers. Recognizing and understanding the moods displayed by pike greatly improves your odds of success by allowing you to adjust your presentations to fit the pike's mood. Keep in mind that not all pike will display the same mood at the same time. A pike's mood can change as quickly as the weather, and daily and seasonal swings are to be expected.

Let's look at one example of a daily mood swing. It's the post-spawn season, and pike of all sizes have gathered near the shallows. The mid-morning sun has started to warm the cool shallows, and the pike begin to become active, but not all at once. Instead, smaller pike become active first, since their bodies warm faster.

At this point, small and medium-sized fish range from neutral to positive, while larger pike are neutral to negative. As the day progresses and the shallows continue to warm, larger pike shift from negative to positive and become aggressive. These daily mood swings in spring are fairly predictable, as long as the weather remains stable.

You'll notice a seasonal mood swing, as spring gives way to summer and the shallows warm beyond the comfort level of bigger pike. Those pike become neutral to negative until cooler water can be found. If large pike can't locate cooler water, they may remain negative for long periods of time and live off their own fat reserves until the water temperature drops again in the fall.

These are two examples of daily and seasonal, temperature-induced mood swings. You'll come across many other factors that affect pike and their moods. These include habitat availability, fluctuating water levels, oxygen levels, and prey availability. Learning to recognize a pike's mood and adjust your presentation to match it is as important as understanding its cause. It's a key factor in making the best of the time you spend on the water.

Overview

Learning how a pike functions within its environment enhances your ability to think like a pike. I don't know of any scientific studies that tell us how fish actually think, but I do know that a fish is more concerned

Learning to recognize a pike's mood and adjust your presentation to match it is a key factor.

with survival and where its next meal will come from than anything else. By knowing what pike require to survive and how they meet those requirements, you can begin to understand the quarry you're pursuing.

By rating the pike's senses in order of importance, you can improve both fly selection and presentation. The lateral line would be first in importance, followed by sight as a close second. Hearing is a distant third, while the senses of smell and taste are not really factors for fly-fishermen. Understanding the role of the pike's senses, you know to design your flies to provide movement and to displace water, as well as to have the shape or silhouette of available food sources.

The pike is blessed with great tools that add to its uncanny ability as a top-end predator—a color scheme that allows it to blend with its environment, a vise-like grip with razor-sharp teeth that spell disaster for any unlucky meal that gets too close, and a body designed for quick bursts of speed. It's no wonder the pike has been around for millions of years. Quite simply, pike are designed to succeed!

In the next chapter, we'll take a closer look at the pike's environment. Like the pike itself, the water it inhabits must also be understood in order to increase your success. Are all lakes created equal? Why do some lakes produce large numbers of trophy fish? When you're fishing a lake with hundreds of bays, which will hold fish?

These are just a few of the questions I'll answer.

TWO

THE PIKE'S ENVIRONMENT

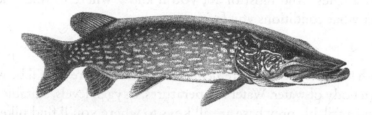

T he next building block in the foundation needed to become a complete pike angler is to learn as much about the pike's environment as you did about the pike itself. The more you understand pike and the world they live in, the more likely you are to succeed in your pursuit of pike, no matter what situation you come across.

Some anglers rely more on luck than they do on hard-core scientific information. While they do have some success, it's sporadic at best, and quite frankly, they're successful on days when almost anyone could catch fish. Some anglers, on the other hand, are very scientific and methodical in their approach, so much so that I've heard some of them described as anal-retentive! Perhaps they are, but they know fish and their environment, and they take that methodical approach with them to the water every day. They're successful with or without Lady Luck on their side.

I'm a firm believer in creating my own luck by knowing as much as I can about the biological and physiological make-up of northern pike and combining that knowledge with a sound understanding of their environment. With these tools, I can be successful on a tough day without relying on luck to bail me out. I can be in the right place at the right time, using the right approach, all based on what I know, not on what I guess! I'll be the first to admit that I welcome any luck I can get, but I believe in bringing knowledge with me to the water first.

That's my pitch to those of you who want to become truly good at fishing for pike with a fly. Now let's take a look at the pike's watery environment. I'll cover lakes in this chapter. River fishing for pike has earned a chapter of its own, and I'll discuss the river's environment in that chapter.

By understanding how a lake functions, you can begin to tie many ideas together to form a basis for your choice of flies, presentations, and strategies. And most of all, you'll know where to find pike, no matter what conditions you face.

All fish have physical requirements that dictate where they'll be within a given body of water. Water temperatures, oxygen levels, suitable habitat, and available prey base are all keys to where you'll find pike.

First, I'll discuss the pike's environment and its habitat preferences, including structure and cover. You'll also need to understand the three life zones of a lake so you can find those suitable habitats. This information will give you a practical approach to choosing the water you'll fish.

After that, I'll discuss lake types, including their seasonal and long-term progression. Knowing lake types will help you anticipate a lake's water clarity, habitat, structure, and cover. It will also help you predict what species of fish are in a lake and even its trophy potential.

You can be successful on a tough day without relying on luck to bail you out.

Finally, I'll take a close look at water temperatures, oxygen levels, lake stratification and turnover periods, and the effects of weather. All of these factors are key elements in the pike's environment, and each plays a major role in determining the location of pike and their moods.

Habitat

The pike's environment can be described simply as its surroundings, which include habitat, structure, and cover. While many anglers assume these three things are one and the same, they're very different. Knowing the differences and how each feature applies to pike is one more piece in your foundation for success.

The wide distribution of pike in the northern climes of North America, Europe, and Russia shows their uncanny ability to survive in a variety of habitats. No matter where you find them, one thing is certain—pike are hell bent on survival. It should come as no surprise that pike are equally at home in rivers, ponds, and large northern lakes.

While pike prefer cool water temperatures, generally between fifty and seventy degrees, they can survive temperatures well into the high seventies and even low eighties. Unlike their cousin, the muskie, and many other fish species, pike can also survive low oxygen levels and do quite well in water with poor clarity and turbid conditions. Pike are present in practically every type of water, from the gin-clear waters of Canada to the muddy, silt-choked Innoko River of Alaska. Pike even inhabit some brackish saltwater areas along the Baltic Sea.

This ability to tolerate a wide range of conditions has made pike a popular choice for stocking outside their natural range in waters where other fish cannot survive. Pike are made to succeed! But that knowledge by itself doesn't tell you much about the specific types of habitat pike occupy.

Pike prefer shallow, dark-bottomed bays and backwater areas that offer quick access to deeper water. Prime pike bays also offer spawning grounds. Another key to preferred habitat areas is the presence of aquatic plants or terrestrial vegetation (flooded land plants). Vegetation offers hiding places from which to ambush prey and provides fish a sense of security. During the spring, pike highly favor bays with a small feeder creek or two. These feeder creeks can carry significantly warmer

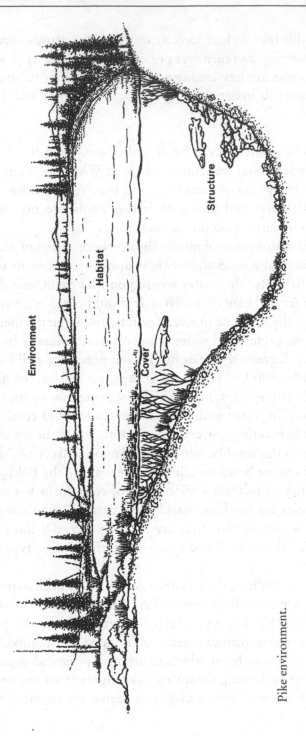

Pike environment.

A key to preferred habitat areas is the presence of aquatic plants or flooded terrestrial vegetation.

During the spring, pike highly favor bays with a small feeder creek.

waters and act as thermal magnets, attracting both prey and pike. These areas are part of the littoral zone of a lake, and I'll talk more about life zones in a moment.

While these habitats are where you'll find pike in the spring, water-temperature preferences overrule structure and cover preferences during the warmer summer months, and larger pike seek out deeper, cooler water. Summer habitat includes areas that have distinct structure—lake points, saddles, rock reefs, and humps with deep water nearby. These areas may or may not have aquatic vegetation, but when vegetation is present, you've found a prime summer pike location. Other summer habitat possibilities include cool- or cold-water sources that may enter the lake via a river, creek, or natural spring. These may be the same feeder creeks that you looked for in the spring to provide water that was warmer than the water in the lake.

In the fall, pike are free to roam the lake as temperatures cool again. You may find them in areas of decaying vegetation in the shallows that they preferred in spring, or you may find them in the areas of structure they occupied in summer. Whatever habitat they're in, there is sure to be an abundant food supply, because they feed heavily in the fall. I'll talk more about seasonal and daily movements in the next chapter.

First, let's look at the two major components of pike habitat—structure and cover. Many anglers confuse these two, but they're distinctly different, and both play vital roles in aiding you in locating and catching pike.

Structure

In fishing terms, structure might best be understood as a change in the contour of the bottom and, as a result, the surrounding depth of water. Structure consists of irregular features, such as points, saddles, humps, holes, and ledges. Other forms of structure include submerged creek channels and even old roadbeds.

A brief description of each of these structures will help you identify them more easily.

Point: land projecting into the lake with shallow water alongside or covering it and deeper water on three sides.

Saddle: a shallow flat that joins separate land masses (islands or an island and the shore) and that is surrounded by deeper water on both sides.

Hump: a bottom protrusion in shallow or deep water that is surrounded by deeper water.

Hole: deeper water that is surrounded by shallower water.

Ledge: a place where a consistent line is formed between shallow water and deeper water and where a distinct change in depth (a drop-off) is present.

———————

Now that you have a basic understanding of structure, how do you find it? Since structure is located underwater in most cases (with the exception of some points and saddle areas), you might not be able to see it easily. Two options are available. If you fish from a boat, you can use a depth finder to locate structure. Depth finders today are so advanced that you can easily locate even deep structure, find appropriate water depths, and even read water temperatures. Depth finders can be invaluable, particularly when you're fishing on large bodies of water.

While this works fine for anglers using boats, those who wade fish are at a disadvantage in locating submerged structure. Not to fear, most lakes now have topographic maps available. These maps easily allow you to pick out structure, including old creek channels. Many of them are so detailed that they even show you where weed beds and other types of cover are located. If a topographic map is available, local shops near a lake are likely to have it. You may have to check with a nearby USGS office; they can often direct you to a retail source for maps.

Fish use structure for many purposes. For instance, they use it as a holding area prior to movement toward the shallows for spawning. Structure is also used as a highway, a place where fish migrate safely from one place to another. On one of my local lakes, an old irrigation ditch that was flooded when the lake was formed acts as one such highway. The ditch is three to five feet deeper than the surrounding area and no wider than six feet, as it snakes its way through the shallow flats. During the post-spawn period, pike use this ditch to filter onto the flats. Its slightly deeper and darker water offers the pike a degree of comfort and safety as they make their way to the shallows.

By learning to identify structure, you can greatly reduce the amount of water you need to cover to locate fish. Areas with structure that also have cover can be primary feeding locations throughout the season. You can fine tune your search for the most productive parts of a lake by finding those areas.

It has been said that deep structure can hold fish without cover, but shallow structure holds few fish without cover. With that in mind, let's take a closer look at cover.

Cover

By definition, cover is something that offers protection. In the fishing world, cover means weed beds, downed timber, rocks, and manmade objects, such as docks, that offer protection, shelter, and a place to hide from prey and predator alike.

Pike are masters of concealment. Whether they're lying motionless on the bottom or suspended in a weed bed, they can be difficult, at best, to see. While many people believe pike to be the bad boy (or girl) on the block—and they are—pike lose their aggressiveness when cover is sparse or absent. Like any other predator, pike rely on the element of surprise, and cover provides it.

The forms of cover I just listed are easily identifiable, but there are others that are equally as important. Wind, muddy water, and cloudy

Pike are masters of concealment.

weather also offer excellent cover that pike make use of when it's available. When wind creates a chop on the surface of a lake, the amount of direct light that penetrates the water is greatly reduced. In turn, this creates cover that the pike gladly take advantage of, as is shown by their aggressive nature during windy weather. Some of my best days fishing have been spent on water where a moderate chop was present.

The wind also creates another form of cover, muddy water caused by wave action. While limiting our ability to sight fish, these conditions create favorable temporary cover from which pike hunt. Sometimes distinct mud lines form, and pike cruise their edges, using them as ambush points.

The last non-conventional cover comes in the form of clouds. Like wind and muddy water, cloud cover limits the amount of light that penetrates the water, creating cover and a sense of security. Cloud cover allows pike to access areas lacking adequate forms of other cover. My favorite cloud cover scenario comes in the form of late afternoon storms that produce low light on flats where little in the way of other cover is available.

Now that we have a basic idea of what habitat, structure, and cover are, let's take a look at the life zones of a lake.

Life Zones

Lakes are complex ecosystems driven by many biological and ecological forces. By better understanding lakes and how these forces affect them, we can begin to predict where pike will be and when they'll be there. The first step is to enter the pike's world and closely examine the lake's life zones.

Freshwater ecosystems such as lakes and ponds are made up of three life zones—the littoral, the limnetic, and the profundal. The littoral zone is the area of the lake where sunlight penetrates to the bottom, allowing aquatic plant life to grow. The littoral zone begins at the shore and extends into the lake to the point where water clarity and depth prevent sunlight from reaching the bottom. The littoral zone also extends out from islands and can be found around shallow-water humps and saddles. In shallow lakes (less than twenty feet), the littoral zone can encompass the entire lake.

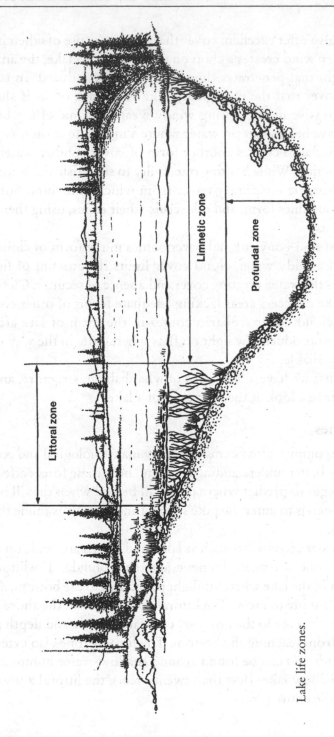

Lake life zones.

The littoral zone is usually the most active area of the lake, because its vegetation attracts all forms of aquatic life. Insects, baitfish, and crustaceans live here. Because it offers cover and food sources, the littoral zone is also the most likely place to find pike in all but the warmest months. It should, therefore, be the zone flyfishermen focus on most.

For pike fly anglers, this is good news, because we're better able to cover water effectively in depths of less than twenty feet. Since the littoral zone is where you'll spend most of your time, recognizing that life zone in a lake helps you eliminate large areas of the lake that simply don't hold actively feeding pike. Littoral areas are easily distinguishable from the other two life zones, allowing you to focus your efforts on the most productive water.

Not all littoral zones are created equal, and the areas that offer the prime pike habitat discussed earlier will hold the most and, with proper temperatures, the biggest pike. The more cover, food, and preferred water temperatures the area offers, the more productive it will be. I had an experience in Colorado that illustrates this very clearly.

I was fishing two bays, which were side by side and faced into the lake the same direction. Both bays seemed identical, with soft, dark bottoms, abundant vegetation, and similar bottom structure, and both offered adequate food sources in the form of crayfish and small suckers. The only difference was that one bay had a small, seemingly insignificant trickle of water feeding into it. It was early summer and water temperatures were on the rise but still on the cool side. Both bays held fish, but one held more and bigger fish than the other.

After a couple of quick temperature readings, I found the bay with the small creek entering it was about five to seven degrees warmer than the other. This temperature difference was key. While I caught fish in both bays, the bay with the small creek offered up four fish between twelve and fifteen pounds, while in the other I only caught a couple of skinny hammer handles and one seven-pound pike. Recognizing subtle differences can reap big rewards.

The limnetic zone is the open-water area of a lake where the sunlight penetrates the surface but does not reach the bottom in sufficient amounts to produce significant plant growth. While this is not a primary feeding area, pike will occasionally be found here when water temperatures or food sources dictate. Even when pike are found here, it's not a prime area for flyfishing because covering deep water is often less productive, since it offers little in the way of cover or structure. There are exceptions that make it a good choice, however.

Large pike will spend time in the limnetic zone if the right conditions exist. During the hot summer months, larger pike are forced out of the shallows by warming water temperatures. Areas where cool water springs seep into the lake draw pike and other fish during these periods. These areas can be totally devoid of plant life and offer little in the way of cover, but they do offer both cool water and an available food source. These two factors attract and hold pike.

On my home waters in Colorado, the large pike have keyed into kokanee salmon, and during the summer months they will follow them into deeper water (as deep as sixty feet) to feed. The pike also find colder, more comfortable water temperatures in the area of the lake where the limnetic zone reaches the profundal zone. These are the times when I've found pike in limnetic zones, but in most cases, the depth at which the pike are holding will severely limit your ability to fish effectively for them with fly tackle.

Deep-water areas of a lake are known as the profundal zone. These areas consist of a soft mud bottom where the combination of low light and low oxygen severely limit the existence of plant life and animals. These areas are typically thirty feet deep or deeper and are not primary feeding areas for pike. It's just as well, since they would be very difficult to fish with fly tackle!

As you learn lake types and combine that with what you know about life zones, you'll begin to know the water you'll want to cover.

Natural Lakes

Over the years, scientists have classified natural lakes into what is known as "trophic states," in order to categorize them according to water clarity, nutrient levels, and algae production. This categorization scheme gives biologists a way to describe and compare the vast numbers of lakes they must keep track of. While it wasn't their intention, scientists also created a useful tool for anglers.

Over the long term, lakes naturally change—they fill with silt, sediment, and organic matter. These materials are washed into lakes by inlet streams and by rainstorms, and they help stimulate the growth of aquatic plant life, creating a more productive ecosystem. At the end of the progression, an overabundance of sediment sometimes makes lakes too shallow to support a healthy fishery. Even though lakes are always changing, each will fit into a category that will help you understand what you might expect and how to fish it.

There are three trophic states—oligotrophic, mesotrophic, and eutrophic. The common denominator in each of these names is "trophic," which relates to a lake's fertility and is also an indicator of its water quality. Oligotrophic translates to few nutrients, mesotrophic means middle levels of nutrients, and eutrophic indicates high nutrient levels.

Being able to recognize a lake's trophic state will provide invaluable information to the angler. By using this classification system, you should, with some degree of accuracy, be able to predict such things as water clarity, bottom makeup, availability of vegetation, what species of fish might be there, and even the potential to find trophy fish. Let's take a closer look at the trophic states and what they mean to us as pike anglers.

Oligotrophic Lakes

Oligotrophic lakes are generally cold, clear, and deep. They usually have low nutrient levels, few areas that offer suitable habitat for aquatic plant life, and steep shorelines with sharp drop-offs. Oligotrophic lakes are capable of maintaining high dissolved-oxygen levels at all depths throughout the year due to their cold water temperatures. The bottoms of these lakes consist mostly of rock and sand with very little sediment build-up.

Due to the steep drop-offs along their shorelines, the littoral zones in these lakes are typically narrow and located close to shore. While you won't find extensive littoral areas, most oligotrophic lakes are large and have lots of shoreline to cover. Oligotrophic lakes offer abundant limnetic and profundal zone areas, but as you now know, these areas are difficult to fish with fly tackle. These lakes can also be very difficult to fish from shore or to wade fish due to the steep banks, so fishing from a boat is often a must.

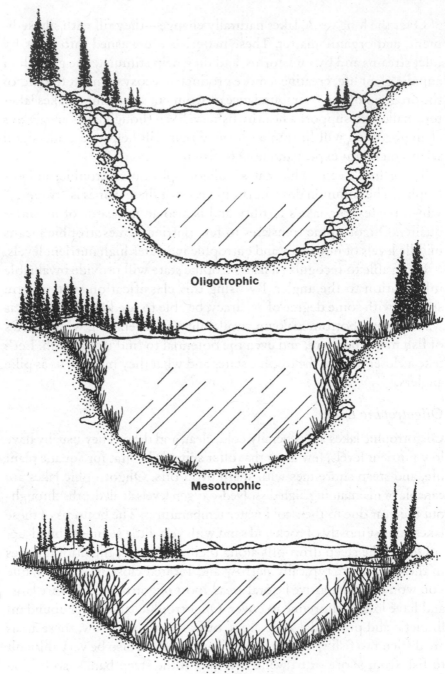

Oligotrophic

Mesotrophic

Lake types.

Eutrophic

Oligotrophic lakes typically support coldwater species, such as trout, and some coolwater species, such as pike and walleye. Pike are native to many oligotrophic lakes. Due to their cold waters, the primary forage base in these lakes consists of fish such as ciscoes and whitefish, and they make up the bulk of the pike's diet. While the deep, cold waters of these lakes make the growing season short, pike in them are capable of living twenty years or more and obtaining gigantic proportions. Some of the largest pike caught each year come from these lakes. However, oligotrophic lakes can support only limited numbers of big pike, and the fishery can be quite sensitive to fishing pressure.

Mesotrophic Lakes

Mesotrophic means "middle nourished" and describes lakes that have a moderate amount of nutrients and moderate water clarity. These lakes have begun to collect sediments along their bottoms, and aquatic plant life has developed. Offering a good mixture of water temperatures and oxygen levels, mesotrophic lakes are in the most stable of the three trophic states. They certainly offer the most diverse fishery, supporting a multitude of species of fish, forage, and aquatic plant life.

The sediments mesotrophic lakes collect create more extensive shallow areas, so the littoral zone extends farther out into the lake. You must be prepared to cover more water in these lakes, because potentially prime pike habitat is abundant.

Pike are native to the majority of northern mesotrophic lakes, and these bodies of water produce more pike than any others. Offering both deep and shallow water, mesotrophic lakes are capable of supporting large populations of pike, while still offering the chance at a true trophy. Of course, the quality of the lake is dependent on available habitat, proper water temperatures, and a good forage base. The overall size of these lakes also has a great deal to do with the pike's success and, ultimately, with ours. The bigger the lake, the more potential for great fishing it has.

The forage base in mesotrophic lakes is usually quite diverse, ranging from ciscoes and whitefish in northern lakes to small bass and perch farther south. Try to check with a local shop or lodge on the lake to learn what forage base is available to pike. This will help you once you hit the water. Find the forage and the habitat, along with proper water temperatures, and you can't go wrong!

Eutrophic Lakes

The richest of the lakes, in terms of nutrients, are eutrophic lakes. These waters are extremely fertile, but there is a downside. Bottom sediment build-up and increased plant and algae growth can create low water clarity. In shallow eutrophic lakes, high water temperatures and low oxygen levels can lead to summer and winter kills.

Pike are native to most northern eutrophic lakes, but small, shallow eutrophic lakes that lack cold-water sources or refuge rarely produce pike of trophy proportions. Pike in this type of eutrophic lake tend to grow much more quickly and, as a result, seldom live long enough to reach their size potential. Remember, the faster pike grow, the shorter their life expectancy is. An old pike in these waters might be ten to twelve years old, while an old pike in an oligotrophic lake might be pushing twenty-five years of age or older.

While large eutrophic lakes may provide all three life zones, you're more likely to encounter vast expanses of the littoral zone and smaller areas of the limnetic zone. Some eutrophic lakes lack a profundal zone altogether. On smaller bodies of water, the littoral zone may cover the entire lake, which makes locating prime pike habitat much like throwing darts while blindfolded. These lakes are the most prone to summer and winter kills from severe temperature and oxygen-level swings. You might expect to find only undersized pike in many of them.

These trophic states describe natural lakes and their progression, but there are many pike fishing opportunities in manmade impoundments. Let's take a closer look at reservoirs and what you might expect to find when you fish them.

Manmade Reservoirs

In discussing manmade reservoirs, I'll give examples from here in Colorado, since I'm most familiar with them, but similar lakes exist throughout much of the country. I strongly recommend contacting your state department of fish and game for information on lakes that contain viable populations of pike.

Here in Colorado many of our manmade lakes are classified as highland reservoirs. These bodies of water are built in mountainous terrain, usually in steep valleys where rivers carved their way through the mountains. Highland reservoirs most closely resemble oligotrophic lakes. They usually have steep shorelines with very little in the way of shallow water. The bottom structure is mostly rock, gravel, and boulders. These lakes may be several hundred feet deep and offer very little in the way of shore- or wade-fishing opportunities. As a result, they're better fished from a boat.

Like natural oligotrophic lakes, there is a very small littoral zone that is normally limited to the immediate shoreline and areas adjacent to islands. These lakes support populations of trout and whitefish. Pike are stocked to control rough fish, or they reach the lake inadvertently from an upstream impoundment.

The largest pike I've seen in Colorado was cruising the steep shoreline of one such lake. This pike was in the mid-fifty-inch range. It was not in a lake known for its pike!

Like natural oligotrophic lakes, these impoundments cannot support large populations of big pike. The occasional monster fish is still taken, but I would not recommend these lakes to those looking for lots of action.

Located on flat valley floors is another kind of manmade lake, one that closely resembles natural mesotrophic lakes. These valley lakes have sloping shorelines with soft-bottomed flats that produce a significant amount of aquatic vegetation. While they have deep water near the dam, the opposite end of these reservoirs often offer ideal pike habitat. Saying that pike do well here would be an understatement. Heated debates at the local Trout Unlimited meetings over pike stocking in these lakes only prove the point.

The three life zones are quite distinct in valley lakes. The littoral zone, with its prime pike habitat, is widespread and offers excellent spawning and feeding grounds. In Colorado these impoundments are our most productive pike fisheries. Elevenmile, Spinney Mountain, and Williams Fork reservoirs all fall into this classification. These prolific pike lakes are also top-notch trout waters. The only negative effect of pike and trout sharing the same waters is when pike deplete other food sources, such as suckers. Then they quickly turn their attention to the trout. Good lake management is necessary to allow the trout fisheries to thrive and maintain a balance. It's a thin line between love and hate here in Colorado.

Lowland reservoirs are located along the eastern and western plains of Colorado. Many of these reservoirs closely resemble eutrophic or, in a few cases, mesotrophic lakes (or somewhere in between). Some of them are quite shallow, less than thirty feet deep, and can suffer from high water temperatures during hot summers and low oxygen levels during unusually prolonged winters. Many of the lakes also become weed-choked during the summer months, and that condition, combined with high summer temperatures, can lead to severe algae blooms, further reducing already low oxygen levels. Summer kills are possible under those circumstances. The littoral zone areas in these lakes can be quite extensive, requiring you to cover lots of water to find areas that hold pike.

The results of pike stocking in these lakes have been mixed. The ability to establish a viable fishery is dependent upon many things, as usual. Pike must have access to cool water, through deep water, springs, or inlets, and the lake must have sufficient oxygen levels, suitable habitat, and a good forage base. The good news is pike are highly adaptive and have learned to survive some of the harsh times in these lakes, as long as there's a period of cooler water temperatures during which they can recover from the harsh summer heat.

Some studies have shown that even when oxygen levels drop dangerously low and water temperatures climb into the low eighties, pike can and do survive. In these conditions, many pike go through what is referred to as "summer stress," becoming quite lethargic and living off their fat reserves. They stop growing and can lose substantial weight. As waters begin to cool with the onset of the winter months, pike become more active, feed again, and put weight back on. It's another good example of how adaptable pike are.

Generally speaking, the biggest drawback to manmade impoundments is water-level fluctuation. This alone can determine how well the pike will do. Reservoirs are typically drawn down during the summer and winter months when pike are most vulnerable to water temperature

The drawback to manmade impoundments is water-level fluctuation.

extremes and low oxygen levels. Pike can have all the food and habitat in the world, but without favorable water temperatures and adequate oxygen levels, it's tough for any fish to survive for long. It's lucky for us that pike are so hellbent on survival!

As you can see, pike live in a variety of different lakes and ponds. Each of these environments varies and so do the density of the population of pike and their ultimate size. One thing can be said, no two lakes are alike and no two lakes ever fish exactly the same. Lakes are complex ecosystems that are constantly changing and so, too, are the fisheries within them.

Water Temperature

All fish are cold-blooded. Their body temperatures are determined by the temperature of the water, and every fish species has a preferred temperature range. As you know, this range is fifty to seventy degrees for pike, with larger pike showing a preference for the cooler end of the range. At temperatures above the preferred range, the pike become stressed and their mood will be negative (inactive). If temperatures fall below the optimum range, the pike's metabolism slows, and once again activity decreases.

Water temperatures vary throughout a lake and its life zones, and they have a direct effect on where fish will be found. Water temperature is only one way to locate pike, but it is probably the easiest. A simple thermometer can help you narrow the search. Remember my earlier story of the two bays that looked identical but didn't fish that way?

Water temperatures also affect the overall quality of a lake's environment, including its physical, biological, and chemical makeup. For example, the decay of dead aquatic plants increases with a rise in temperature, and the bacteria that feed on the decomposing material consume oxygen, altering the dissolved oxygen available to pike. This can create areas of oxygen depletion, which pike and other fish avoid.

Pike, like all fish, seek a balance that allows them not only to survive but to thrive, but water temperatures are only one part of the puzzle. Other factors, such as food availability, may cause pike to leave their comfort zone—if only for short periods—to feed.

Consistent success depends on your ability to locate areas where pike spend a great deal of their time. Using your understanding of habitat, adequate forage, and favorable water temperatures and oxygen levels will increase your success. Be aware of the many variables and be flexible in your approach to finding pike.

The Oxygen/Temperature Connection

A discussion of water temperature and its effect on a lake's ecosystem would not be complete without a more detailed look at dissolved oxygen and its role. The temperature of the water determines the amount of oxygen that can be dissolved and held in the water, as well as the rate of photosynthesis in aquatic plant life in the lake's littoral zone. Without oxygen, of course, lakes cannot support life. Fish, insects, and zooplankton all consume oxygen and give off carbon dioxide.

Levels of dissolved oxygen are measured in parts per million (ppm). Different species of fish require different levels of oxygen for long-term survival. Fish such as trout require colder, more oxygenated water in the range of 3.0 ppm to 5.0 ppm, while warmwater fish such as carp can survive in warm, turbid waters where oxygen levels may be as low as 1.0 ppm.

So where do pike fit in? Somewhere in the middle. Remember, a pike's preferred water temperature varies with its size. While small pike can survive a wider range of water temperatures and oxygen levels, big pike show a definite preference for cooler, more highly oxygenated waters. The listed minimum requirement for long-term survival of pike is around 1.5 ppm, slightly above carp and bullheads. These are minimum requirements, and pike do better at levels above the low end of the scale.

Aquatic plants and algae produce oxygen by photosynthesis during the day. These same organisms consume oxygen during the night. This causes fluctuations in the amount of dissolved oxygen available. The littoral zones in lakes with extensive aquatic plant life can have extreme swings. Areas with high oxygen levels that hold lots of fish by day may have levels so low during the night and dawn hours that those fish must move. This fact alone may begin to shed some light on the daily movements of pike. Combine it with water temperature changes and the movement of forage fish and you should really begin to understand why pike aren't always where you expect them.

The effects of changing water temperatures and dissolved oxygen levels don't happen instantaneously. Pike move gradually from deep to shallow water in the morning and gradually from shallow to deep as night approaches. There are only two things that cause abrupt movements—extremely stormy weather and the arrival of the trout-stocking truck.

Many factors determine water temperatures and the resulting oxygen levels, including daily and seasonal warming, weather, and water entering the lake from a river or spring. Two seasonal events, lake stratification and turnover, are also major factors.

Lake Stratification and Turnover

Water reaches its peak density at thirty-nine degrees Fahrenheit. Water that is either warmer or colder cannot sink below a layer of water of that temperature. Temperature differences within a lake can keep water from mixing, creating stratification of a lake. Ever been swimming in a lake where the water is warm in the shallows, but as you wade out in slightly deeper water, you can feel cold water on your feet? This is an example of how water forms distinct layers based on temperature.

Stratification occurs during the summer and, to a lesser extent, again during the winter months. Lakes and ponds that are less than twenty feet deep may never stratify, since their waters continue to mix all year. These are the same lakes and ponds, by the way, that can suffer from summer and winter kills, because there's no place for fish to seek relief.

During the summer stratification, there are three distinct temperature layers in a lake. The epilimnion is the uppermost level, and it is the warmest. The next layer is the metalimnion. The lower part of this cooler, middle layer contains the lake's thermocline, where water stops mixing and sharp temperature drops begin.

Below the thermocline is the hypolimnion, where the water temperatures are sharply lower than those of the two upper layers. Due to the density of its water, the hypolimnion does not mix with the upper two layers. The thermocline can be a key factor in locating and finding summertime pike or any other species of fish trying to find cooler waters. The more distinct the temperature layers are, the more important this factor becomes. One thing you should know is that the three layers are not uniform in thickness. They can also vary throughout the season and even on a daily basis. Wind and weather, for instance, can quickly affect the thickness of the layers.

During the summer season, the epilimnion will reach its maximum depth, usually around twenty feet. Summer stratification is then in effect and will hold until the fall turnover period. Wind circulates the surface water and causes some mixing of the epilimnion and the uppermost layer of the metalimnion, but those layers of warmer water cannot penetrate the colder, denser water of the hypolimnion. When the epilimnion warms too much for coolwater species such as pike, they seek deeper water where cooler temperatures and higher oxygen levels offer relief. Understanding stratification provides great insight into summer pike locations, particularly in the case of larger pike.

If you were to look at a horizontal cutaway of a lake during summer stratification and then overlay the three life zones, you'd really start to understand how the lake's ecosystem works. The relationship between the littoral zone and the epilimnion layer would be particularly clear. In the littoral zone, you can see the plant life, feel the water

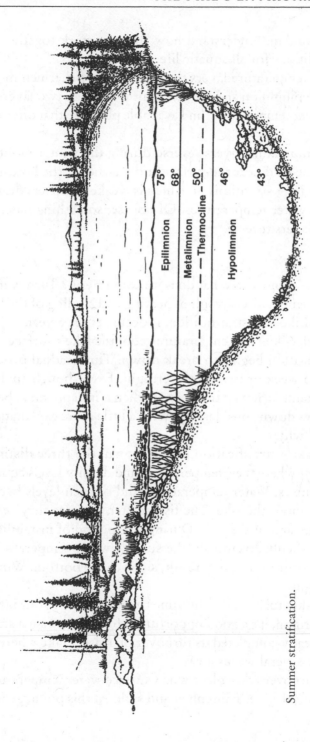

Epilimnion

75°
68°

Metalimnion

Thermocline—50°

46°

Hypolimnion

43°

Summer stratification.

temperatures, and understand how the two work together to create prime conditions for all aquatic life.

The two temperature layers that concern flyfishermen most are, of course, the epilimnion and the metalimnion. These two layers have the oxygen, water temperatures, and available plant life that offer pike what they need.

Water-temperature layers reverse during the winter months, when lakes become cold near the surface and warmer at the bottom. This is known as winter stratification, which is weaker with less dramatic differences in water temperatures. Of course, something has to happen before the layers reverse.

Turnover

What is lake turnover? What does it mean to you? Turnover is a phenomenon that is a direct result of heating and cooling of the lake's surface water. Like lake stratification, it occurs twice a year.

In the fall, colder air temperatures cool the lake's surface, and summer stratification begins to break down. This gradual process takes place over a week or two, not overnight. Even though anglers might not understand turnover, they know when it is happening, because the fishing slows down considerably. With a little more explanation, you'll understand why.

As the lake's stratification breaks down, the three distinct layers reach a point where their temperatures and density levels equal out and the water mixes. Water temperatures and oxygen levels become uniform throughout the lake. The fish scatter, because they're now able to access all parts of the lake. During this period of instability, fishing becomes difficult. Eventually the surface water temperature reaches thirty-nine degrees and, as a result, sinks to the bottom. Winter stratification begins.

Not all lakes turn over at the same time, and when your favorite lake is in this turmoil, it's a good opportunity for you to visit a smaller lake that has already completed its turnover or a larger lake where turnover may still be several weeks away.

Spring turnover takes place when surface water temperatures warm to thirty-nine degrees Fahrenheit and sink. At this point, general water mixing occurs and water temperatures are uniform from top to bottom. Turnover recycles the lake's nutrients that settled on the bottom over the winter months. Concurrent with this, waters warm and spring winds begin to blow, mixing those nutrients and creating oxygen levels that are moderate to high throughout the system.

After the spring turnover, the lake begins to blossom with new life. Soon the water begins to stratify again, distinct temperature layers form, and all the lake's creatures find their niche, which makes locating pike a lot easier.

I've experienced good fishing before and after both turnover periods, but fishing during turnover is slow at best. As I mentioned before, it's a good time to check out some other lakes.

Weather Effects

At first glance, stillwater fisheries appear to be just that—still. Nothing could be further from the truth. We've discussed turnover, when there is lots of movement of water within a lake. Wind can also have a dramatic effect on stillwaters by creating currents and stacking the lake's water on the downwind side. Wind is a vital part of everyday life in lakes.

Wind is the primary agent in the mixing and oxygenating of the top layer of water during summer stratification. While it's vital to the fish population, wind also creates direct benefits for the fisherman. Wind pushes the warm surface water and stacks it on the downwind side of the lake. When water temperatures in the lake are still a little on the cool side, you'll find pike on that downwind side.

When the water is too warm, wind can also help. As the wind pushes surface water toward the downwind side of the lake, cooler water near the bottom of the epilimnion layer is forced to the surface on the upwind side. This circulation process can create differences in temperatures as small as one or two degrees or as much as eight to ten degrees. The greater the difference in temperatures, the more dramatic the effect is. Fishing the upwind side of a lake on days when the overall surface water temperatures are high can mean the difference between success and failure.

Currents are also generated by wind, and they create feeding areas. Tiny insects swept by wind-induced currents and pushed into concentrated areas draw baitfish in to feed on them. Pike will then slide in to

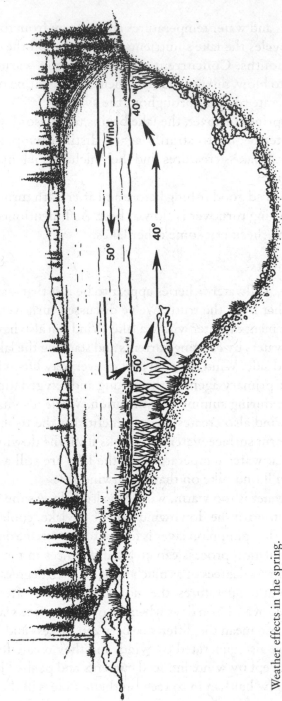

Weather effects in the spring.

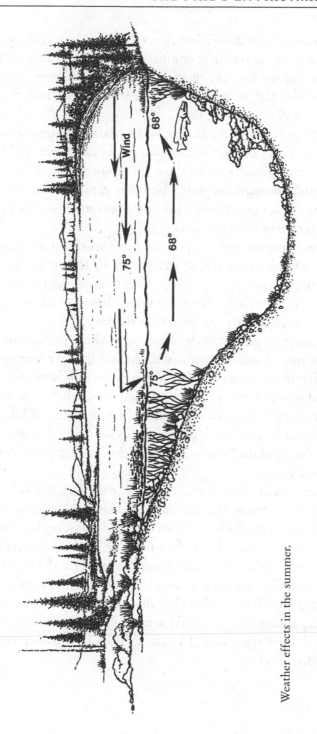

Weather effects in the summer.

take advantage of this dinner line, as well. This is one of those situations where pike might leave their comfort zone and venture into warmer or cooler water for the sake of an easy meal. Wind-generated currents can also be charged with highly oxygenated water, and if conditions dictate, that will also draw pike.

Main lake points and saddles between islands are important feeding areas during windy times. Saddles create a funnel effect, and fish gather on the downwind sides to feed on the assorted food items that are swept through the narrows. Any place that attracts fish is sure to attract larger fish to feed upon them. This point was made clear to me several years ago on a trip to Manitoba.

It was midsummer and the pike had dropped out of shallow water and scattered among emergent weed beds in about ten feet of water. While fishing was steady, we were having to cover lots of water to keep the action constant. Early afternoon winds began to blow and soon became very strong as they swept across the lake.

In an attempt to get out of the wind, my fishing partner and I slipped behind a series of small islands. We noticed that we were picking up fish only around the cuts between the islands, nowhere else. Whitefish had moved into the cuts to feed on small insects being swept through them. That, in turn, drew the attention of nearby pike. While we caught the occasional fish in other places, the saddle areas were the honey holes. As the wind died down, the fish slowly dispersed, returning to their normal haunts.

I've experienced similar success on the downwind side of points, particularly long points that extend for a distance under shallow water and then drop off abruptly. As with the saddles around the islands, fish take up positions along the downwind side of these points to capture food being pushed along in the current created by the wind.

One other effect often overlooked by anglers is that wind creates chop on the water. You'll remember that this helps create cover by reducing light levels, giving fish an added sense of security, making them less spooky and more aggressive. I'll take a choppy lake over a smooth-as-glass lake any day!

The saddle areas were the honey holes.

By now I hope you're beginning to appreciate the complexity of the factors that affect pike and the flyfishermen who seek them. And I hope you're not too overwhelmed by it. It's the relationship between life zones, lake stratification, water temperatures, and available oxygen that is the key to helping you locate pike. Any one of these by itself doesn't tell the story, but as you start to piece together all the factors and experience them in your own flyfishing, you'll get a much clearer picture. But there's still more information we need to consider.

In Colorado it's often said that if you don't like the weather, wait ten minutes and it will change. Two weeks ago I was sitting here writing and stealing the occasional glance outside as snow piled up by the foot. This morning I'm watching thunderstorms roll by. So goes the weather in Colorado. So too goes the fishing, when we factor in the effects of the weather.

Lakes are at their most sensitive as they shed their winter blues. Spring days begin to warm the littoral zones of the lakes, and then, just as fish begin to move out of the depths and aquatic vegetation begins to bloom, Mother Nature throws us a curve ball with the return of Old Man Winter. When this happens, pike retreat from the shallows where we like to fish for them. The severity of the front and the swing in temperatures determine how long their retreat will last.

When fishing for ice-out pike in Canada, I've seen bays that were so choked with pike you could walk across their backs be totally devoid of fish the next day. Air temperatures dropped twenty degrees in less than twelve hours, while the shallow water the pike were in dropped close to ten degrees. This drove the pike to deeper water where temperatures were still unaffected by the cold front.

If the weather remains cold longer than a couple of days, it will, of course, take longer to warm the shallows back up. Should rain or even snow accompany a cold front, conditions can change even more rapidly and take even longer to bounce back. Luckily most spring storms are short-lived, and their effects usually don't last more than a day or two. I'll discuss tactics to deal with these situations in the chapter on presentations.

Another spring phenomenon worth considering is that water levels in most lakes begin rising. Snow melt and spring storms sometimes cause water levels to rise very quickly. This creates new habitat that might be suitable for pike in the form of submerged land vegetation, which means there's more water to cover.

As spring gives way to summer, lakes stratify. When this happens, fish and their locations become more predictable. Weather conditions can now work in our favor, as summer thunderstorms and gusty winds provide brief periods when the fish leave deeper water for shallow water to feed again. Remember the keys to locating pike during summer stratification conditions and the isolated good fishing spots the wind can create? Cloud cover and rain can also help to cool surface temperatures enough to allow brief forays into those areas, and winds that churn the surface increase available oxygen levels.

In the time leading up to fall turnover, waters begin to cool and this can draw baitfish and pike back into shallow water areas. Keep in mind that once the turnover is complete, the pike can follow their available prey source anywhere, whether it is deep or shallow. I'll discuss the pike's seasonal movements in the next chapter.

Overview

The water that the pike calls home has its own biological and physical makeup. Knowing a lake's trophic state can tell you, sight unseen,

When fishing the ice-out in Canada, I've seen bays so choked with pike you could walk across their backs.

Cloud cover and rain cool surface temperatures enough to allow brief forays into the shallows.

many things about its health, condition, bottom makeup, water clarity, and even what species of fish are likely to be found there.

Knowing the life zones—littoral, limnetic, and profundal—and what role they play in a lake's ecosystem, can tell you what types of habitat, water temperatures, and fish we will find in each of them, allowing you to eliminate large portions of the lake that rarely, if ever, hold actively feeding pike. You know now that it's a pretty safe bet that the littoral zone of a mesotrophic lake, for example, will be a good place to find and catch some pike.

You've also learned the effects of lake stratification and turnover on the location and movements of fish. By knowing the pike's temperature preferences, you can predict where they'll be with a simple thermometer.

Of course, you know there has to be more. To help you locate pike on a truly consistent basis, you must understand the daily and seasonal movements of pike. Then you'll have a wide base of scientific information to complement your luck the next time you go fishing.

THREE

SEASONAL MOVEMENTS

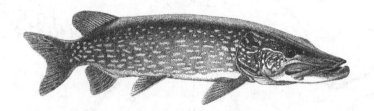

Pike have a seasonal calendar that is determined by many factors, including the spawn, food sources, available habitat, and water temperatures. For pike, the seasons are marked by movements. They move from deep water to shallow in spring, from shallow back to deeper water in summer, and then to shallow water again in fall. Finally they return to deeper water for the winter season, and we return to our fly-tying desks.

As we look at each season, we'll also take a look at the daily movements of pike. Understanding seasonal and daily movements will help you locate pike and choose the best presentations to use.

These migrations are progressive in nature, and their timing varies from one lake to another and sometimes between areas of the same lake. As usual, many factors determine timing. Initial movements into the shallows in spring, for example, occur according to the size of the fish, with smaller pike normally showing up first. They're also the last to leave when summer temperatures cause pike to move to deeper water.

Besides the size of the fish, pike migrations are also directly affected by changing water levels, unsettled weather, available food, and suitable habitat. These factors, alone or in combination, can hasten, slow, or even postpone pike movements. Luckily, these effects are typically short-lived, lasting a couple of days. In extreme cases, such as wide fluctuations in water levels, several weeks might pass before the pike's seasonal movement is complete and the fishing stabilizes.

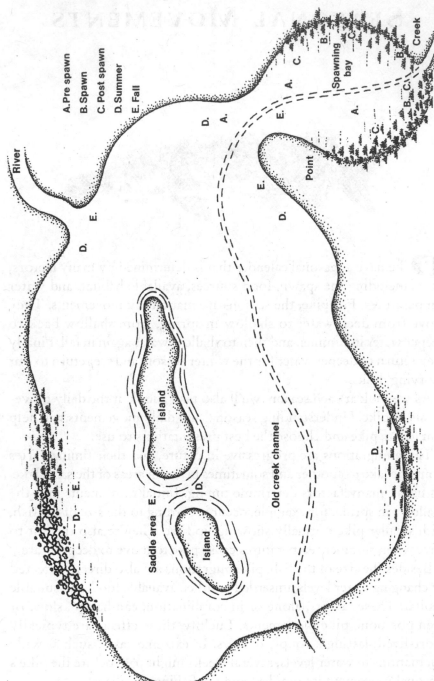

A. Pre spawn
B. Spawn
C. Post spawn
D. Summer
E. Fall

River

Creek

Spawning bay

Point

Island

Island

Saddle area

Old creek channel

Lake seasonal movements.

The type of lake you're fishing also determines seasonal movements of pike. For example, eutrophic lakes, shallow by nature, warm faster in spring than deep, steep-sloped oligotrophic lakes, while mesotrophic lakes fall somewhere in the middle. The overall size and depth of the lake also determines how quickly it warms. All this should explain why pike in one lake you fish regularly might be spawning while pike in a nearby lake may still be in the pre-spawn stage.

It has been said that ten percent of the water holds ninety percent of the fish. Eliminating unproductive water by using your understanding of lake types, life zones, and the other factors that affect the seasonal and daily movements of pike will give you more time fishing prime water.

Let's look at the northern pike's calendar in detail. The spring season really has three parts, and I'll describe each of them, followed by the summer and fall seasons. I'll also discuss daily movements within each period. We'll examine all the factors that impact these movements. While the problem looks complex at first, you'll learn quickly how to eliminate water that holds little hope and focus on prime water during the three seasons we can catch pike. Let's take a journey with old *Esox* as it moves through those seasons.

Spring: Pre-spawn

With the onset of spring, the ice slowly recedes along a lake's edge, and the lake begins to come to life. Adult northern pike begin to migrate from their winter haunts in nearby deeper water to warmer, shallow-water, back-bay spawning areas. These areas warm more quickly than the main lake, usually becoming ice-free long before the ice breaks on the deeper water. The pre-spawn movement is the first migration pike make, and it's the most reliable. The spawning urge is very strong.

My first experience with pre-spawn pike fishing came while I was trying to shake the winter blues and sneak in some early-season trout fishing. I was somewhat shocked when I arrived at the lake to find it still nearly covered with ice. The only open water was a sliver along the shallow, southern shoreline where small feeder creeks dumped into the lake. There might have been twenty to thirty feet of open water between the shore and the receding edge of rotting ice. Since I'd driven

With the onset of spring, the ice slowly recedes along a lake's edge, and the lake begins to come to life.

a long way to get there, I thought I'd at least give it a try. I will never forget the rest of that day.

I rigged up my seven-weight rod with some 3X tippet and picked out an assortment of Clouser Minnows. I'd fished these patterns during previous ice-outs for the lake's sizable brown trout and occasional lake trout, and I'd done quite well. After fishing for several hours and picking up a couple of nice trout along a point, I made my way into a small back bay. I noticed that the water where a small creek entered the lake had opened up nicely as the spring sun continued to warm the air and, more importantly, the water.

Until this outing, my Colorado pike fishing typically didn't start until mid- to late May during the post-spawn period. To be honest with you, the thought of catching pike that day hadn't entered my mind. However, as I got closer to the creek inlet, things started to get interesting. One cast after another met with a strong take followed by limp line. After losing several flies, I checked my leader carefully, fearing it was bad. The leader was fine. On closer examination, I noticed that the leader had been cut clean with no nicks and no abrasions. The only logical answer was ... pike!

I walked back to my vehicle, found some steel leader, and returned to the place where the assaults on my monofilament leader had taken place. My next cast put the fly within inches of the ice. I counted down, allowing my Clouser Minnow to sink nearly to the bottom. My slow, steady retrieve brought an abrupt strike, and I was quickly into a heavy fish. After several tense moments during which the fish made runs under the jagged edge of the ice, a magnificent pike of over forty-five inches and twenty-five pounds rested in the water at my feet.

The remainder of that afternoon's fishing resulted in a total of seven fish, all pike and all over fifteen pounds. The two largest fish stretched the tape to forty-five and forty-six inches, and both weighed twenty-five pounds. It was quite a welcome to pre-spawn pike fishing. Big fish and big fun!

I think you'll now understand why early-season quickly became one of my favorite times of year to fish for pike. If you're willing to battle the annoyances of early spring—cold weather and temperamental fish—the payoff will come in the form of giant-sized pike!

The payoff will come in the form of giant-sized pike!

Water Temperatures

Water temperature is critical during the pre-spawn, more so than at any other time of the year. It determines the location of pike and the timing of their movements, and your success as a fly-rod angler at this time of year is dependent on understanding the effect of water temperature.

The pre-spawn movement starts when temperatures reach about thirty-nine degrees, depending on your location. Sunny, warm spring days produce the best results. The sun and warming air temperatures heat the bays first, and pike slowly filter out of deeper water into the flats. This solar heating is critical to these shallow-water deployments and the pike's willingness to chase your fly. With water temperatures on the cold side early in the day, you'll find the pike to be lethargic, their mood neutral to negative. Mornings are better used to scout areas or sneak in some trout fishing.

Typically water temperatures increase as the day progresses, and by the afternoon, the pike's mood shifts from neutral to positive. As their body temperatures rise, they become more active and aggressive, and they'll be more eager to chase your flies.

Solar heating is critical to the pike's willingness to chase your fly.

Location Keys

Using what we know about water temperatures and the pike's mood, let's take a closer look at keys to finding the pike's location. Pre-spawn pike, both large females and the smaller males, will stage along the structure created by the first drop-off adjacent to spawning bays. Old creek channels, troughs, and breaks in bottom contour also provide structure where shallow water meets deep. They serve as pike highways. Pike filter through them into back-bay spawning locations, so you should fish these areas and the adjacent flats first, prospecting for pike moving into the back bays. Later you'll move on to fishing the bays.

Not all back-bay spawning areas are created equal! Remember that the best have key features that separate them from the rest—a soft, dark bottom, aquatic or terrestrial vegetation, and a small feeder creek. The dark bottom absorbs the sun's heat significantly better than rocky or sandy bottoms and supports the aquatic plant life that pike need for spawning. The feeder creeks act as thermal magnets, typically carrying water that is significantly warmer than the bay and drawing pike toward them.

While not as critical, bays with necked-down openings also offer an advantage over bays with wide openings into the main lake. The water in necked-down bays is typically shallower and warms more quickly. The wind can stack warmer surface water into these bays, and they'll hold the warmer water better and longer, because their waters don't mix back into the general lake water the way the waters in an open bay do. For this reason, I always try to fish the downwind side of the lake at this time of year. Warmer water always attracts anxious spring pike. And it's not just pike that are attracted to these warmer areas—forage fish are also drawn to them.

Daily Movements

The daily movements of pike at this time of year vary as much as the weather does. While warm, stable weather produces conditions that permit afternoon movement into the shallows, cooler weather keeps pike holding tight to the bottom in their staging areas. Little or no movement toward the shallows will take place. The pike's general mood during these periods is neutral to negative, and you'll find them sticking to structure or cover, reluctant to move far. Severe cold fronts can put the fish down for several days until warmer, more stable weather arrives. Even then, it may take a few more days before pike return to the shallows.

As you might expect, these daily movements are based on many factors besides water temperatures, and they vary between lakes and within each lake. The pre-spawn period lasts from ice-off until spawning commences. In Colorado this period is from about mid-March through the first part of April in the lowland lakes, and mid-April through the first part of May in our mountain lakes.

Pre-spawn Tactics

Flyfishing for pre-spawn pike requires several tactics. Remember that your efforts should be focused during the afternoon hours when pike are most active. Start your pre-spawn day in the late morning hours outside bays, along the structure created by the first drop-off. From there, work the old creek channels and other pike "highways," progressing into the bay itself as the afternoon sun heats up.

For fishing the drop-offs and creek channels, use a sink-tip line and a weighted pattern, such as a Clouser's Half-and-Half, which will allow you to probe the drop-offs more effectively.

During the pike's transition from deep to shallow, switch flies to a deer-hair diver, such as an Umpqua Pike Fly or a Dahlberg Diver. Continue fishing these flies with your sink-tip line, because this allows you to present the fly in a vertical column of water to locate the fish. This is a crossover technique from conventional angling, the equivalent of using a neutral-density jerkbait. A sink-tip line and a diver can be a deadly combination for pike that are beginning to feed actively but aren't yet highly aggressive.

By the time you reach the shallows, the pike will have had time to warm their chilled bodies and will be more willing to chase the fly, and your technique should change again. Switch to a floating line and throw a Bunny Fly or large Deceiver, although the sink-tip line and diver combination will still work well.

If the fish aren't willing to chase your first offering, you can often counter their lethargy by getting your fly down in front of them and working it slow. Try a Dahlberg Diver again, using a sink-tip or full-sink line and a short leader. Get the fly down to the bottom and use quick tugs to dig it into the muck. If this still fails to entice a response, try a Clouser Half-and-Half and jig fish it by bouncing it along the muck with pauses between the strips.

Spring: Spawn and Post-spawn

As a time of transition, the pre-spawn is short-lived, but it's great fishing. Soon the spawn will be on and the brief, intense feeding period that preceded it will cease. The big female pike shut down and turn their attention toward perpetuating their species. Smaller males can still be caught, and while not all the pike spawn at once, action slows to a crawl, at best, during the spawn.

During this time, my advice is to leave the pike to their business and go fish for something else. But before we do that, there are important things we can learn from spawning pike.

Even though the spawn itself offers poor fishing, the information it gives us is invaluable for our success in locating and tracking pike throughout the remainder of the season. First, it tells us where the pike are in their seasonal calendar and gives us fair warning that post-spawn fishing is coming up. Second, the spawn offers clues as to where we can find pike during that great post-spawn period.

As water temperatures stabilize in the thirty-nine to forty-five degree range, pike will be spawning. As you'll recall, they'll be in the dark, mucky-bottomed, back-bay areas you've been fishing during the pre-spawn. A small feeder creek is a plus, as is vegetation to spawn over. The larger female pike broadcast eggs over the vegetation, as one or more smaller males fertilize them. This routine is repeated daily over a three- to five-day period.

Once the spawn is complete, the females depart for parts unknown to recuperate from its rigors. They return to the shallows in a week or two and rejoin the males in and around the spawning areas. This time they're ready to feed and replenish weight lost during the spawn. This is one of the most coveted times in flyfishing for pike.

The post-spawn period is what pike flyfishing is all about. Large numbers of pike in assorted sizes—including the big ones—are gathered in relatively small areas in shallow water, and their mood is now super aggressive. This is great news for the flyfisher, because pike will take a variety of offerings. If you're a streamer fisherman, then fish streamers. If you like the heart-pounding excitement of top-water action, throw poppers and divers. No matter what flies you use, now is the time for some fast and furious fishing.

Some of my greatest days of pike fishing have happened during the post-spawn period. One memorable day, my partner and I cut through a small necked-down opening in our boat, rounding a tree-lined point to find a bay that the pike gods must have created. It was a large bay that averaged maybe three feet in depth. Several small feeder creeks dumped into the back of it.

The bottom was dark and soft but still suitable for wading. Water clarity was good, and although the tea-colored water was still cool, it was on the upward swing. Newly sprouting vegetation was beginning to reach the surface. Was this the perfect pike bay? Only time and the pike themselves would tell!

If you like the heart-pounding excitement of top-water action, throw poppers and divers.

Parking the boat just inside the cut, we quickly discussed how to approach the bay. Winning the coin toss but deferring to the "second half," my partner offered me first choice. Bad mistake. Those who've fished with me have given me the nickname of Hoover! They know I leave little behind as I work a lake. I positioned myself just off the shoreline, leaving my partner the deeper water. My first cast told me we'd hit the pike equivalent of pay dirt.

I put my Bunny Fly in a small opening between some flooded rice grasses, and the surface of the water grew "excited." One strip of the fly and wakes erupted from the nearby shoreline like torpedoes homing in on an ill-fated cargo ship. One more strip and all hell broke loose! No less than a half-dozen, trophy-sized pike were in an all-out sprint to see which would get there first.

Fish actually fighting over your fly! These are the things all anglers dream of. We spent the next four hours fishing that bay and caught a total of thirty-nine fish over forty inches, with the largest stretching the tape to almost fifty inches. Welcome to pike-fishing nirvana, welcome to post-spawn pike flyfishing!

Water Temperatures

While the locations you'll find pike are the same for the pre-spawn and post-spawn periods, water temperatures and food sources dictate their daily movements and are still key to locating pike. In the shallows, the temperatures will now vary between fifty-five and sixty-five degrees, the pike's preferred temperature range. That helps explain why all sizes of pike are found together at this special time of year.

While lake temperatures are beginning to stabilize, they're still at the mercy of late spring cold fronts. When these storms are strong enough to drop water temperatures, they can drive pike from the shallows for brief periods.

The overall mood of the pike is now aggressive and will remain so, as long as water temperatures and water levels remain stable. Add in prime habitat and a good forage base, and life is good for the pike. That's reflected by their sheer numbers and their aggressiveness. The key to continued good fortunes for pike and angler alike is stability within the system. Abrupt changes can still throw you a curve ball and severely affect the pike's daily movements and mood.

Daily Movements

One afternoon, I overheard a conversation between several anglers after a successful post-spawn pike outing. They were making plans to return the following morning and fish the same spot. Sorry guys, it doesn't work that way!

Understanding the pike's daily movements during this time of year is very important. Movement into the shallows is temperature induced, as it is during the pre-spawn. And like the pre-spawn, daytime warming waters draw pike into the shallows, while cooling waters push them back out to deeper water for the night. Again, the afternoon bite will probably be better, as bigger pike continue to filter in throughout the day.

The other factor in daily post-spawn movements is, again, the weather. Cold weather can greatly restrict the pike's movement into the shallows, especially early in the season. Temperatures can drop quickly in the shallows, forcing pike to retreat to deeper, warmer water. These late-spring weather changes are usually short-lived, and the pike return once the waters warm or the weather stabilizes.

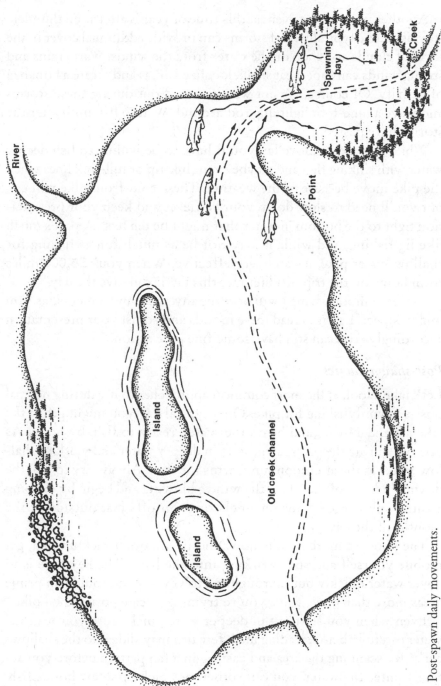

Post-spawn daily movements.

Another noteworthy event at this time of year is afternoon thunderstorms. These typically brief storms can provide additional cover in the form of clouds and chop on the water from the winds. Warm rains and strong winds can superheat small, localized areas and create a bonanza of activity. Of course, it's not wise to stand out during these storms and wave a nine-foot lightning rod around. Wait to fish until after the storms have passed.

While they don't move far, you'll have to be willing to fish deeper water with sinking flies and maybe even sink-tip or full-sink lines when the pike move because of the weather. These cold-front pike will eat, but you'll need to slow down your retrieves and keep your presentation tight to the bottom in water that might be ten feet deep. It's much like jig fishing, and while it may not be as much fun as fishing for shallow-water pike, it's still very effective. When you're 3,000 miles from home on the trip of a lifetime, this tactic can save the day.

Extreme mood swings will accompany these movements, as you might expect. Learn to read these moods and adjust your presentation accordingly. You can still have some fine pike action.

Post-spawn Tactics

Let's take a look at the most common approaches to use during normal post-spawn flyfishing for pike. On a typical day you might get to the lake around 11 a.m. and be on the water, ready to fish, by noon. As you did during the pre-spawn, start in deeper water and work to shallow water as the afternoon sun warms the flats. Always try to fish the downwind side of the lake if the wind's blowing and begin by probing around submerged creek channels or drop-offs just outside of the mouths of the bays.

The pike are more mobile now, and if you don't pick up fish, get mobile yourself and start working into the bays. The key here is to cover water quickly but thoroughly. However, you should fish prime areas more than once, while you're trying to locate post-spawn pike.

Even when you start out in deeper water, make sure you scan the water carefully before wading in. A few fish may slide into the shallows early. By scanning the area and casting in a fan pattern before you actually enter the water, you can sometimes pick up a few bonus fish.

Start in deeper water and work to shallow water as the afternoon sun warms the flats.

This only takes a few minutes to do, and you'll avoid spooking good fish because you've assumed they're in deeper water.

At this time of year, I primarily use floating lines and large Bunny Fly streamers under normal conditions. Day in and day out, I take the bulk of my pike with large subsurface streamers, such as the Bunny Fly, and I'd recommend you start with this setup, too. Keep your retrieves slow and deliberate, with four- to six-inch strips being the norm. As the day moves along and pike activity increases, so should the size and speed of your retrieves. As a general tactic, you should constantly vary your retrieves until you discover the mood of the pike and what trips their trigger.

By mid- to late afternoon, you should have moved into the backs of the bays. At this point, you may opt to throw top-water flies like poppers and divers. Don't hesitate to experiment until you find the right combination of lines, flies, and retrieves. I'll talk more in detail about these tactics in the presentations chapter.

Summer

Like all good things, the post-spawn period must come to an end. As we move into the dog days of summer, the shallows warm beyond the comfort level of larger pike, and they retreat to deeper, cooler climes.

This happens over a period of time. In my home waters of Colorado, this movement usually takes place during the last few weeks in June, as the surface temperature pushes seventy degrees. Know your waters and follow their temperatures, as every lake is different.

Small pike may remain in shallow water throughout the summer months, because they can tolerate warm water better than their bigger brothers and sisters. Large pike are forced out of the shallows, and if you still wish to pursue them in the summer months, you must move with them.

Pike in mesotrophic and eutrophic lakes, with their extensive flats, may have to move far from shore to find cooler water. Oligotrophic lakes, with their steep shorelines and quick access to deeper water, may hold big fish tighter to shore longer into the summer. Often, they also offer shallow rock reefs where larger pike may hold throughout the season.

Water Temperatures

When the water temperature in the shallows approaches the seventy-degree mark, all but the smaller pike have retreated to deeper water that is not only more comfortable for them but also for the fish they feed upon. The aquatic weeds in the shallows that were just springing to life a month ago are now in full bloom and reaching the surface. This offers excellent summertime pike habitat along the first drop-off where there is quick access to deep water. These areas are usually no more than a couple of hundred yards from the same bays where pike spawned earlier in the season.

Drop-offs and rock reefs are your first jumping-off points, as you search for summertime pike. A good topographic map will help you locate submerged weed flats with sharp drop-offs. Describing this in terms of the lake's life zones, you are looking for areas at the edge of the littoral zone where it meets the limnetic (open water) zone of the lake. In simple terms, you're looking for the area of the lake where the shallows meet deeper, more open water.

Location Keys

Location keys for summer pike are as varied as the lakes they live in. Depending on what is available, pike will be found on weedy, mid-depth flats adjacent to deep water or on rock reefs and saddles between islands. These areas will hold fish from summer through the fall months.

Other keys include cold-water sources, such as springs. With their constant water temperatures, these springs are the same ones that attracted pike in the springtime because their waters were warmer than the lake's water. Now they offer water that is cooler than the lake's summer temperatures.

Another key to consider is lake stratification. Summer lake stratification offers distinct temperature layers, and fish seeking out cooler water will vacate the upper layer (epilimnion) and drop into the cooler middle layer (metalimnion) where water temperatures are more to their liking. Understand that pike will leave these areas, if only briefly, to follow their food sources. Once the feed is over, they'll return to their comfort zone.

Daily Movements

Besides brief moves to follow forage fish during the day, the pike's daily movements in summer include early-morning and late-evening forays into the shallows when food sources dictate and water temperatures permit. I have to warn against using water temperatures as your only guide to where pike will be during this time. I provide water temperatures as a general guide, because it's the easiest factor to measure, but there is much more to the equation.

You must also consider habitat in the form of structure and cover, but more importantly, you must understand where the pike's food is located. In all but special cases, such as the spawn, food will override temperatures and cover. Pike will leave their comfort zone to follow their food. Knowing the pike's preferred forage in the lake you're fishing is of great importance. In one Colorado lake, the largest of the pike disappeared every summer, and no one was quite sure where they went. We all had our ideas, but it wasn't until a couple of kokanee salmon fishermen reported being bit off by pike in sixty feet of water that we had our answer. The pike followed the schools of salmon to deep water and remained with them until the fall salmon run brought them back to the shallows.

No matter what your local pike forage base is, it pays to become familiar with *their* habits and tendencies, as well as the pike's. By understanding the pike's food source, you'll begin to anticipate the patterns of your local pike. When you can consider all the information, not just the easy things such as water temperature, then, and only then, will all the pieces of the puzzle begin to fit together and make sense.

Summer Tactics

My summertime tactics for pike include the use of a boat, either a belly boat or regular fishing boat. Either one allows me to cover more water, which is necessary since the pike are scattered along the edges of the weedlines and drop-offs. Wade fishing is basically over until the fall months, when pike will return to the shallows and be within reach of shoreline anglers again. Some far-northern lakes, however, may offer shallow-water flyfishing throughout the summer. Summer is also a great time to fish rivers, as you'll find out in the next chapter.

Your approach to summer pike should be to start out in the mornings by probing the inside and outside edges of deep-water weed beds and main lake points where pike concentrate. You should also fish the same submerged creek channels that you did in the spring, this time in slightly deeper water. Like deep-water weed beds, these areas offer substantial weed growth, as well as cooler water. Last, but not least, explore river mouths where they dump into a lake, offering another source of cool water. You can see why boats are an important tool. Your success will be measured by how much water you can effectively cover.

As the day progresses, move out and fish rock reefs and points, as well as saddles between islands. During the summer months, you should use sink-tip and full-sink fly lines, as you probe deep along the drop-offs and weed beds. Since you'll be fishing deep water, weighted flies, such as the Clouser's Half-and-Half and the Blanton's Flashtail Whistler, should be your first choice.

You'll be fishing on or near the bottom most of the time, but sometimes pike will hold between the bottom and the surface. For these suspended pike, you can incorporate the use of diving-type flies with sink-tip lines and long leaders. This tactic allows you to fish a column of water, seeking the level where the fish hold by experimenting with wait times and retrieval speed.

One of my favorite summertime tactics is to fish the downwind side of cuts between islands on days when there's a stiff wind blowing. As you'll remember, pike gather on the downwind side to feed on the bait-fish that have gathered there to feed on the insects being swept through these areas. A potential bonanza awaits the summertime pike angler lucky enough to be in the right place at the right time. Knowing to check these areas should help you create your own luck.

Fall

Fall is big-pike time! The waters have begun to cool, and the big girls are free to roam about the lake once again. Not since late spring have the truly big pike been easily accessible to the fly-rod angler. In fact, the only pitfall I can find to fall pike fishing is that the pike can be anywhere and, at times, everywhere! Familiarity with the forage base of the lake and the habitat pike use will help you focus on some specific areas for fall pike.

Water Temperatures

The cooling of water as summer begins to fade dictates another move for pike, and it's essential to understand it in order to be successful in the fall. As the lake's summer stratification breaks down and water temperatures become more uniform, all fish, not just pike, begin to re-locate. If the pike in your lake are eating perch, then they will follow the schools of perch to their fall, deep-water haunts. Suckers and trout, however, will move to shallow water, and if they're the main item on the menu, pike will now be able to follow them there.

Knowledge of the pike's requirements as it prepares for the upcoming winter will help you. Food is the primary factor in locating fall pike! If you know where the pike's food source is located, chances are the pike won't be far behind.

The pike's general mood at this time of year is positive, dictated by the need to put on weight before the winter months set in. This is the last big feed, and pike must prepare for the long winter and the following spring's spawn. This situation makes for a very good scenario for the pike angler—big pike feeding with purpose!

Location Keys

Key locations for fall pike include rock reefs, saddles between islands, main lake points, and old, decaying weed beds. I consistently have had my best luck fishing around reefs and saddle areas that have some weed growth visible and are located near primary and secondary bays. If these key areas offer deep water nearby, they're even better!

Daily Movements

Daily movements of pike in the fall can be extremely unpredictable, with forage availability the key factor. Be prepared to cover lots of water. I move often, jumping from weed beds to rock piles and back. I have no magic answer here other than to focus on the prime areas I've described and combine that with an understanding of what the pike are feeding on. Like any other time of year, don't be afraid to cover prime water more than once. Remember the pike are mobile, so you should be, too.

cult.

Fall Tactics

Fall pike days should find you exploring those prime areas armed with a sink-tip or full-sink fly line, a short, three- to five-foot leader, and a fly of sizable proportions. Fall pike are looking for a big meal, if they can find one. Oversized #5/0 Lefty's Deceivers and Bunny Flies are the norm. Your retrieval should be slow and steady for best results.

You should typically start your day by probing the inside and outside edges of weed beds located outside a main bay. Only work your way inside the bay after all outlying areas have been fished. If these locations fail to produce, search out rock reefs and saddles where some vegetation is visible. These areas are best fished from the outside in. Fishing from deep to shallow over rocky areas produces the best results. Keep in mind that these areas are most productive when they offer quick access to deep water.

Overcast days with a good chop on the water provide ideal fall weather conditions, and pike will be active throughout the day. Work the downwind side of whatever structure or cover you're fishing. As we've discussed, pike will be in those places as food is pushed toward them. Cover these areas thoroughly and always check nearby open water, as well.

I catch my biggest fish, year-in and year-out, during the fall. This time of year is best described by saying, "It's not quantity, but quality."

But if you're willing to do your homework, fish high-probability areas, and cover water, there is no reason why you can't have both. Go ahead, it's okay to spoil yourself and have the best of both worlds—quantity *and* quality.

As the waters continue to chill, the first ice can't be far behind, and the pike season draws to a close. The last time I checked, nobody had come up with a way to catch pike on the fly through the ice, so it's time to prep your tackle and get flies tied for next year. Pre-spawn isn't that far away!

As we move into the next chapter, I'll discuss what rivers have to offer the pike angler and why certain times of year I'd rather leave the still-waters behind and move with the current. Let's go check out river pike!

I catch my biggest fish, year-in and year-out, during the fall.

RIVER PIKE

My first experience flyfishing for pike in a river was twenty years ago. That trip was very successful, but it still took me ten years to return to fish for pike in a river. You might wonder why.

Like most anglers, I had some preconceived notions. I believed that in order to find the most consistent action and the biggest fish, I should be fishing lakes, preferably big lakes. Big mistake was more like it! I've since learned that, by not fishing rivers, I was missing some of the most prolific big-pike waters North America has to offer.

Many of the top pike waters in Europe are rivers, and those waters produce some of the largest pike caught every year. Meanwhile, flyfishers in North America rarely pay much attention to fishing rivers for pike. When I tell people I'm going pike fishing, they just assume I'm heading for a lake. Few realize the potential of these practically unfished waters, not to mention the trophy possibilities. I hope this chapter teaches you to know better!

Flyfishing for pike in rivers offers some distinct advantages for those of us who just can't get enough of chasing pike. For one thing, water temperatures don't typically fluctuate the way they do in lakes, providing more reliable fishing. In summer, when pike are forced to deep water in lakes, sometimes out of reach of the flyfisher, rivers offer a great alternative. Fall offers another advantage when low water levels in rivers concentrate pike, allowing you to focus on select locations.

Few realize the potential of rivers, not to mention the trophy possibilities.

Of course, there are some disadvantages. The main one is high water levels during spring run-off and after unusually heavy summer rains. These fluctuations cause river pike to scatter, making them difficult to locate, but you can often overcome this by floating the river to cover more water.

Do river pike grow as big as pike found in lakes? In many cases, they grow bigger! One look at the record books clearly shows this. Six of the current International Game Fish Association world records were caught in rivers! Three of the other records came from lakes that are, in actuality, large, sprawling river systems that have spread out over time to form lakes.

In Europe, river pike reach mammoth proportions, growing to weights in excess of forty pounds. My personal best pike of fifty-three inches came from a river. The fact is, I've now taken eleven pike over the magical fifty-inch mark, and nine of them came from rivers. River pike do reach trophy proportions, and the fact remains that most pike rivers are virtually unfished. So you'll understand, I've had to overcome some degree of selfishness to share the story of river pike with you.

Pike River Characteristics

A number of factors contribute to the making of a good pike river. The size of the river, the speed and depth of the current, access to interconnected lakes, sloughs, or other backwater areas, the amount of cover available, the water clarity, the food sources—all these factors and more determine a pike river's quality. Good pike rivers have positive features in several of these categories, while great pike rivers have them in all.

Over the years, I've had the opportunity to fish some of the best pike rivers in North America. At the end of this chapter, I'll list some of the most productive of them. Right now, I'd like to introduce you to one of my favorite pike rivers, as we break down the characteristics of a pike river in detail.

The Innoko River in west central Alaska has a tremendous reputation for world-class pike flyfishing. Wide-bodied and slow moving, this large river snakes its way through low wetlands. Hundreds of interconnected lakes and large backwater sloughs are part of its features.

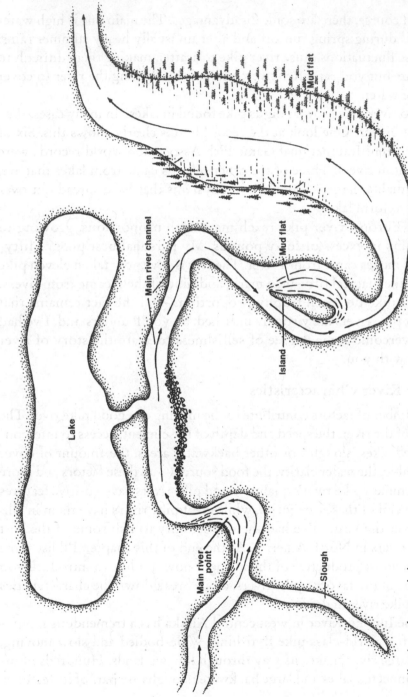

Pike river characteristics.

The Innoko River in west central Alaska has a tremendous reputation for world-class pike flyfishing.

In the spring, pike use these areas as spawning grounds, and during high-water periods throughout the rest of the season, they provide feeding areas.

Lack of a strong current greatly benefits pike in the Innoko. Pike like slow-moving, flat rivers, where they can hold and wait to ambush their next meal without having to expend energy fighting the current. Steep-gradient rivers favored by trout are not beneficial to pike. Unlike trout, pike simply aren't built to fight current.

Structure and cover come in many forms on the Innoko, offering pike ideal ambush locations and great holding areas for resting. Shallow-water mud flats, saddles near islands and oxbows, and hundreds of thousands of flooded trees are present. Even when pike are forced out of their favorite backwater areas into the main river, they have excellent habitat. While the Innoko does not offer the abundance of aquatic weed growth you might find in other rivers, it does offer the occasional collection of lily pads and, during high-water periods, vast areas of flooded grasses, both of which provide excellent feeding grounds.

The Innoko has main and secondary points similar to those we find in lakes, and pike hold near these areas. Main river points are formed where sediment collects at sharp bends and at the ends of islands. Over time, sediment build-up creates flats that extend out into the river, and they provide excellent feeding areas for hungry pike with easy access to deeper water. These are excellent summer and fall locations for pike.

Secondary points are basically smaller versions of main points. They're most commonly located adjacent to lake and slough mouths. While these areas are considerably smaller and typically do not hold numbers of fish, they're always worth fishing, since they attract the occasional monster. Pike hold in these areas as they move in and out of the lakes and sloughs and as they migrate up and down the river.

Water clarity also plays a role. Off-color water offers pike additional cover for hunting and added security to roam more freely. Under these conditions, pike rely more heavily on their lateral line than their keen eyesight. It's a fair trade for the tactical advantages discolored water provides.

Given the choice of fishing a clear river or a discolored one, such as the Innoko, I'll take the dirty water every time. Pike are considerably more aggressive and are less prone to follow and inspect a fly in dirty

Secondary points are commonly located adjacent to lake and slough mouths.

water. Instead they're forced to use their lateral line to locate a meal and then make a quick decision on whether to eat it before they lose track of it.

Another key factor for greatness in pike rivers is how much and what kind of food is available. Adequate food sources are critical. In the Innoko River, pike feed on sheefish, salmon smolt, and whitefish at different times of the year. As I've emphasized, knowing which food is available and where the food will be in the river helps immensely in locating pike. In the Innoko, for instance, pike feed heavily on sheefish and whitefish during the spring and early summer months. But in the fall, they take advantage of the tremendous run of salmon smolt migrating to the ocean.

In some Canadian rivers, pike feed on walleye, grayling, ciscoes, and suckers. In Colorado, they may feed on minnows, suckers, and trout. Whatever the forage is, there needs to be an adequate base to make it a good pike river.

Seasonal Movements

Northern pike living in rivers go through seasonal changes, just as they do in lakes. Seasonal movements are again driven by water temperature, available food, and habitat.

Water temperatures in river systems are typically more stable than in lakes. Temperature stratification, for instance, is much weaker than it is in lakes, if it occurs at all. This stability helps keep pike in their comfort zone throughout the season and allows them access to all parts of the river at almost any time, and that means that covering large amounts of water is often necessary. That presents its own set of problems.

In Colorado we have the Yampa River, which has limited access by foot. That means floating the river is necessary in most situations. On the Innoko River, its sheer size makes a power boat a must. You use the boat to access areas and then wade fish, but you'll still need a boat. Over the years, this method has served me well as it allows me access to good fishing areas, plus the opportunity to wade fish to cover the water thoroughly.

Southern rivers have bigger temperature swings than the rivers of Alaska and the northern parts of Canada. In rivers where higher water

Colorado's Yampa River has limited access by foot, and floating the river is necessary.

temperatures affect the location of pike, I seek out side streams and other sources of cooler water that attract fish, just as I do in lakes. Overall, water levels, available forage, and habitat affect the location of pike in rivers more than water temperatures.

While water temperatures are fairly stable in rivers, water levels are not. Fluctuations in water levels cause significant changes in the location of pike, no matter what the season. In two- to three-week periods fishing the Innoko, I've experienced the direct effects of changing water levels at different times of year. During rising waters, pike scatter as new locations become available. Fishing is least predictable during this period. Falling water causes pike to pull out of shallow areas and retreat to deeper water. Once again, fishing becomes unpredictable.

Stability is the key. High water or low water—I really don't care. But please give me stability. With high but stable water levels, I'll find pike in the river's connecting lakes and sloughs. Low but stable water levels move pike to lake and slough mouths and into the main river.

Slow, subtle changes in water levels are not as much of a problem as sudden changes, whether the river is rising or falling. Slowly changing conditions will not cause pike to abandon their locations overnight. When change happens over a period of weeks, it's much easier to track the movements of pike.

As we examine the seasons of river pike, you'll notice that the tactics you use and the locations of pike don't change much. There are subtle differences, but with stable water temperatures, pike can access all parts of the river all season, and you'll fish for them in much the same manner.

Spring: Pre-spawn

During the time leading up to ice-off, pike gather at lake and slough mouths, sometimes in incredible numbers. Driven by hunger and the urge to spawn, pike begin to shake their winter blues, and these staging areas offer flyfishers their first crack at river pike. This is true trophy time, but it comes with a price—timing is critical and often unpredictable. The season is full of promise, but the possibility of disappointment is high.

In a perfect world the ice would break and allow for several weeks of pre-spawn pike fishing; in reality it rarely happens that way.

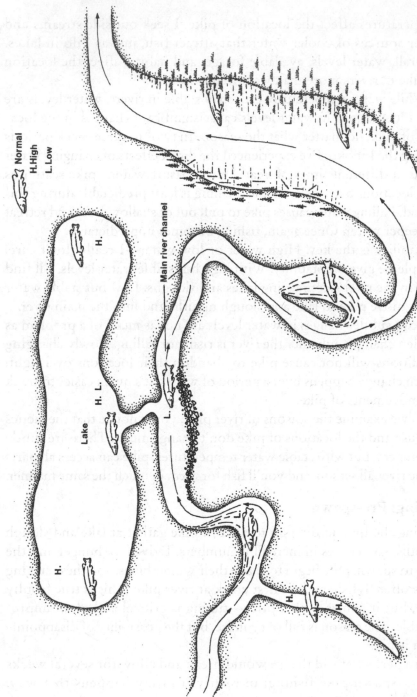

Normal
H.High
L.Low

Main river channel

Lake

Typical river pike locations.

When the ice breaks on a river, the lakes that feed it won't be far behind. When the ice goes off the lakes, high waters are usually close behind, as snowmelt begins to flood the river.

For me, fishing for pre-spawn pike in rivers isn't worth the risk of disappointment, and I usually opt to fish lakes until the post-spawn period. Lakes are much more predictable early in the year, and I feel my time and energy is better spent on them.

In the rare event that you should find fishable water at this time of year or if you have no other choice, your first option is to explore flooded backwater areas of the river's sloughs and lakes. Here you'll locate water that will be a little friendlier than the rushing torrents and severely discolored water the main river will surely offer.

Water Temperatures

The water at this time of year is cold, of course. A river will often be colder than nearby lakes. Water temperatures of thirty-five to forty degrees are to be expected during the pre-spawn. Again, I urge you to seek out backwater areas where warming waters can help concentrate pike.

Sun and warming air temperatures heat the sloughs and flooded flats first, and pike slowly filter into these areas as the day progresses. As with lakes, the early morning hours tend to be fruitless and better spent scouting water or fishing for something else. Water temperature is especially critical to your success, so pay special attention to your thermometer and seek out the warmest water you can find.

In Colorado, we have pike rivers that receive water released from reservoirs. That water is usually warmer and can create isolated hot spots (in terms of water temperatures *and* fishing success), where pike will gather in large numbers and can be quite aggressive. You usually can't count on releases, but if you fish rivers below reservoirs, it's another factor to consider. The winter months can be an excellent time to look for warm-water springs. Water near these springs rarely freezes. Take notes and return there in spring.

Location Keys

Pike begin to stage at sloughs and lake mouths adjacent to spawning grounds. You should first probe likely-looking structure in the form of main and secondary river points near those grounds, before you move into the lakes and sloughs.

Great spawning areas in lakes are relatively easy to identify, and pike are concentrated in them, making their location fairly predictable. In rivers there are large areas of suitable spawning habitat spread out over many miles. Because river pike make use of what's available in their neighborhood during the high-water spawning period, you must investigate areas such as a flooded farmer's field next to the Yampa River or a backwater slough on the Innoko that is bone dry other times of the year. You'll have to cover more water as the river rises and new areas become available to the pike. Lakes and sloughs with extensive aquatic or flooded terrestrial vegetation are favored as spawning areas, and they should be explored first.

Daily Movements

Pre-spawn river pike hold overnight in deep water adjacent to lake and slough mouths. As waters warm, they slowly filter into the flats and

In rivers there are large areas of suitable spawning habitat spread out over many miles.

flooded areas. These daily moves are temperature induced and progressive in nature. Don't show up at 9 a.m. and expect to find pike in the shallows. Instead, start your day around noon when the water has had a chance to warm.

Explore main and secondary points located near spawning areas first and then progress with the pike as they slowly move toward the lake and slough mouths. Cover these areas thoroughly before fishing the lakes or sloughs themselves. Try to mimic the pike's daily movements!

With water temperatures being key, cold fronts can create havoc by preventing pike from making afternoon forays into the shallows. Instead, they'll hold in deeper water throughout the day and are much less aggressive. When this happens, expect slow fishing for several days until warmer, more stable weather returns.

Pre-spawn Tactics

As you start your day in the late morning, probe the deep-water edges of those main and secondary points at the mouths of lakes and sloughs using a full-sink or sink-tip line rigged with a short leader of five feet or less and a weighted fly. The Clouser's Half-and-Half and a weighted version of a Flashtail Whistler are good choices.

As water temperatures warm, move with the pike as they begin to filter into the sloughs or spread out onto flooded flats. Now you should use a sink-tip line with large, deer-hair divers. This deadly combination has accounted for many big fish along the edge where deep water meets the shallows. If this fails to produce, switch to a Bunny Fly or a large Deceiver before venturing farther into the shallows. By doing this, you can be confident you've covered the water column.

Once you've reached the back of the sloughs or flooded flats, change to a floating line and a large Bunny Fly. Pike here have had time to warm up and should begin to feed aggressively. Varying your retrieve is important, and you should constantly try new speeds and movements until you've found what the pike want. Even at its best, fly-fishing for spring pike can be frustrating. You're likely to have many follows without strikes. Patience and the willingness to make presentations using different combinations of lines and flies at varying retrieval speeds are necessary.

Spring: Spawn and Post-spawn

Just as in lake fishing, fishing during the spawn is just not worth the effort. The pike are focused on spawning, and while smaller males can still be taken, the bigger females shut down. Quite frankly, you're better off fishing for other species.

While the spawn itself offers slow action, you can gain information that will be invaluable. For instance, you can discover new areas to fish during the post-spawn period and during the next year's pre-spawn. Be warned, however, that rivers fluctuate more than lakes do, and as a river begins to recede from its spring high-water mark, some spawning areas may not be available to pike for the rest of the year.

During the post-spawn, there's a real difference between fishing lakes and fishing rivers. In lakes, pike are concentrated in specific areas during this time of year, making them easy to locate. Rivers, on the other hand, can still be high, offering pike large expanses of favorable habitat and keeping them scattered in comparison. The fishing is still excellent, as the pike are highly aggressive, but you have to be prepared to cover lots of water.

Would I pass up a chance to fish for post-spawn pike in a high river? No, but given the choice, I'll take post-spawn pike in a lake every time. Lakes are more predictable than rivers at this time of year and so are the pike. Much of our success in rivers is dependent on water level and strength of flow, and I've experienced the highs and lows of pike fishing in rivers during this prized season.

In good years, the river recedes back within its banks and flow levels return to normal. The pike are concentrated in typical post-spawn locations, much as you'd find them in lakes. On the other hand, in years when there is unusually high snow pack or extremely wet weather, high water may last throughout the post-spawn, keeping the pike scattered. When conditions are right in rivers, they can rival the best pike lakes anywhere, but chances are the conditions will be less than perfect.

My best post-spawn river experience took place in northern Manitoba in late June. We had heard rumors of great fishing on a neighboring lake. Getting there would require us to run the full length of the lake we were fishing, some forty miles, plus another twelve miles of river. Knowing the neighboring lake had little pressure and a reputation for producing monster pike, we decided it was worth the time and effort.

After several hours, we made our way from the main lake into the river. We pulled off into a large slough to refuel the boat and stretch a bit from our long journey. As the boat drifted along, I saw several nice pike, one after the other. It was noon, and the thought that I hadn't wet a line, much less caught a pike, crossed my mind. I asked my guide if he minded if we fished this slough as long as we were already there.

He looked at me, smiled, and said, "You just can't get enough of this, can you?"

Grinning back, I just raised my eyebrows and shrugged my shoulders.

In an attempt to stretch both my fly line and myself, I cast as far across the slough as I could. What happened next explains why I began to pay attention to rivers. As I started my retrieve, I felt an abrupt jolt and was quickly into a good pike. What got my attention here was not the fish I had on, but a second pike that intently wanted the fly the first one had eaten. Once landed, my fish stretched the tape to forty-six inches, but the other pike would have been in the mid-fifties. The larger fish simply disappeared into the dark water while we quickly tried to unhook the first one and get a cast off to it.

While we never did get the big fish back up, we did mange to take another half-dozen pike in the mid-forties out of the back part of the slough. Feeling like a kid in a candy shop, I asked my guide if there were any more sloughs like this along the way. Hundreds, he replied.

If there's one thing I've learned about fishing it is this: don't leave a place where there are big fish in order to get to a place where there's supposed to be big fish! Continuing up the river, we fished every nook and cranny. The bigger the slough, the more fish it held. The next thing we knew, it was time to head back. Our tally stood at over 100 fish, with thirty-two of those fish over forty inches. The largest was a beautiful forty-eight-inch pike with a twenty-one-inch girth!

Were there big pike in the lake we were so anxious to reach? Don't know; we never got there! We were quite content with the river and the pike we found there. The fact is that we were in the right place at the right time.

The largest was a beautiful forty-eight-inch pike with a twenty-one-inch girth.

Water Temperatures

Water temperatures and food sources are still keys to locating river pike, just as they are in lakes. While there may not be large temperature swings, variances can still be found and will help you find prime holding water.

Water temperatures in rivers during this time of year often run about ten degrees cooler than in lakes, from forty-five to fifty-five degrees in most northern river systems. Even a minor increase in temperature will attract pike. Small feeder creeks, for instance, can carry warmer water and create good holding areas.

Since rivers don't have the temperature swings lakes do, weather has a less dramatic effect on the fishing. However, storms that produce lots of moisture can have an immediate effect. Whether in lakes or rivers, stability is preferable to change. I don't mind foul weather, as long as it's consistently foul!

While fishing the Innoko River over a fourteen-day period, we experienced one day of sunshine followed by thirteen days of cold rain. The first day produced excellent fishing. Three days of rather poor fishing ensued. Once water temperatures stabilized, even though the cold rain continued, the pike returned in numbers and good fishing returned as well. During the first day, we found water temperatures in the low sixties. After two days of cold rain, water temperatures dropped into the mid-fifties. By the fifth day, the temperature had stabilized at fifty-three degrees, and the bite was on. Stability is key!

Location Keys

During the post-spawn, river pike make daily movements in and out of the shallows, much as they do in lakes. These movements are progressive and vary, depending on the usual factors: water temperatures, available habitat, water levels, and food sources. In the early part of the period, pike spend a great deal of time in fairly shallow water. As the post-spawn progresses and summer approaches, pike spend more time in or near the main river and only make the occasional foray into the shallows when food is present.

I like to subdivide the post-spawn period in rivers into thirds—early, middle, and late post-spawn. During the early post-spawn, start your days at the mouths of lakes and sloughs and along secondary points located nearby. As the day progresses, move back into the lakes and sloughs and fish them until you run out of water. Areas of flooded vegetation are a definite bonus when they're available. Mid- to late afternoon will typically find the pike sunning themselves in the shallowest water, sometimes in water so shallow their tails stick out of the water, creating a scene that looks like oversized bonefish on a saltwater flat.

In the middle part of the post-spawn, there's a slow transition during which pike spend less and less time in the shallows. This is particularly true of big pike. When this happens, key locations again include the areas inside and outside the mouths of lakes and sloughs. Main and secondary river points located close to lakes or sloughs are also key. Don't give up completely on the shallows, but if you fail to locate many big fish there, focus on these other areas.

By the late part of the post-spawn period, pike spend even more time in the main river and deeper parts of the lakes and sloughs. Sloughs and small lakes can get warm enough in summer to push big pike out of them altogether. At this time of year, pike have a strong tendency to feed in the main river and then pull into these areas only late in the day to digest their meals.

On a recent late post-spawn outing I found pike feeding aggressively in the river along river points within several hundred yards of the lakes and sloughs they'd favored several weeks earlier. Late each day the feeding would slow and the pike would disappear. Curious to see where they were going, I slowly approached one of the lakes. I could see pike scattered along the shoreline leading into the lake. As I entered the lake, I was astounded to see literally hundreds of pike stacked in the shallows near the shore.

The problem was that the pike were not there to feed, as I found out after several frustrating hours of throwing flies to countless big pike that refused to eat. These pike had full bellies and had simply pulled into these slack-water areas, where warmer waters aided their digestion.

During the late post-spawn, you should focus your attention on lake and slough mouths, main and secondary points, and mud flats and islands in the main river. Again, the locations favored by pike in the late post-spawn offer easy access to the lakes and sloughs they now use as a giant sofa after a big meal. As fishing begins to slow each day, you should always explore these areas. While these fish aren't actively feeding, you can usually tempt one or two of them into having a light snack on top of their main course. In an area holding several hundred fish, you might catch only two or three fish, but it's not a bad way to end the day.

Daily Movements

In rivers, pike hold in deeper water in and around the mouths of sloughs and other backwater areas. They filter into those areas as food sources dictate and water temperatures permit. Again, the afternoon bite will be better than the morning hours.

Weather can be a factor in daily movements, but since rivers tend to be cooler than lakes, cold fronts have less of an effect. However, river levels rise and fall much more quickly from heavy rains, and that creates disruptions in the pike's movements. It may take from several days to several weeks for things to return to normal.

The good news here is that when conditions force movement, river pike rarely move far. They typically take up temporary residence in slightly deeper water along the inside and outside edges of the mouths of sloughs and side channels. Other key areas to focus on are islands and the mid-depth flats near them. Main river points where flats extend some distance underwater often hold numbers of pike during cold fronts.

As in lake fishing, you'll have to be willing to cover deeper water, getting your fly down five to eight feet. Often this requires a full-sink line and weighted flies with slow retrieves. Cover the water thoroughly before proceeding into the sloughs or lakes. Keep in mind that as the post-spawn period nears its end, pike spend more time in the main river.

Post-spawn Tactics

In the mornings, you should probe the inside and outside edges of lake and slough mouths first, as usual. Next try main and secondary points located near those mouths. You'll need to fish these areas with a full-sink or, at the very least, a sink-tip line. Preferred fly patterns include the Clouser's Half-and-Half and weighted Whistler patterns. Success in the early part of the day depends on your ability to fish deep-water structure where it gives way to shallower water.

You should next make your way inside sloughs and side channels and work toward the back of these areas. The timing of your move into these areas changes as the post-spawn progresses. In the early post-spawn, you should be working toward the back areas in early afternoon. In the middle post-spawn period, and you'll be working them later in the afternoon. Finally, in the late post-spawn, pike are in those areas even later, if at all, and they're there basically to digest their meals.

As you work inside the sloughs, switch to a floating line and a large streamer, such as the Bunny Fly. This is my favorite shallow-water combination, since the fly rides in the top twelve inches of water and stays free of snags. Start your retrieves slow but steady, with four- to six-inch strips. Vary the retrieval speed and length of the strips until you find the right combination.

As the afternoon progresses, you should work tighter to the shore-lines, sometimes in literally inches of water. As I mentioned, pike will be in water that is so shallow parts of their bodies are actually exposed. The hardest thing to do when you see pike in water this shallow is to maintain your composure and figure out which end to cast to. During the early post-spawn, these fish will still be actively feeding. In the middle and late post-spawn, they may only be resting and digesting their meals. Even at these times, it's worth a try.

My favorite way to fish, again, is to throw large Bunny Flies while probing the edges of flooded grasses and downed timber. I switch to deer-hair divers and poppers when casting into heavy vegetation.

As I said earlier, the post-spawn period is a time of transition. Pike spend less and less time in the back areas of lakes and sloughs and more time in the main river where they'll stay most of the summer.

Summer

Flyfishing for pike in lakes is not much fun when summer water temperatures force them to retreat to deep water, but rivers are great places to fish for pike in summer. If water levels remain high enough, pike are still in the shallows. Any retreat is caused more by receding water levels than rising temperatures. Most often, however, run-off swollen rivers have shrunk by summer, forcing pike into the main river channel. Either way, they're still more accessible than summer pike in lakes.

My favorite rivers are ones that link a series of interconnecting lakes, channels, and sloughs that contain enough water and are cool enough to hold summer pike. These rivers are home to lots of big fish in fairly shallow water throughout the season. Even if pike are forced out of shallow water, they seldom move far.

Most northern Canadian and Alaskan river systems fit this description and offer excellent pike flyfishing throughout the hot summer months and into the fall. When I set up my trips for the upcoming pike season, I plan to fish lakes during the pre- and post-spawn and river systems during the summer and fall months. Good, consistent pike fishing revolves around stability. Summer and early fall typically offer the most stable conditions in rivers.

Water Temperatures

With water temperatures in the fifty-five to sixty-five degree range in many rivers, pike can be almost anywhere during the summer months. With fairly consistent water temperatures and levels, food and habitat play a more significant role in where pike are found during the dog days.

Unusually warm summers in the Far North can drive pike from a river's smaller lakes and sloughs. I've occasionally seen water temperatures in these areas reach the low seventies, forcing pike to retreat to the main river, but it doesn't happen very often or last for very long. On a recent trip to Canada, I found water temperatures in the low sixties. Within five days, water temperatures fell into the high forties. Swings like this are unusual during summer, but they still throw a monkey wrench into the best-laid plans. When it comes to rivers in the Far North, be prepared for all possible scenarios. Most of the time, you'll find stable water temps and levels, allowing you to focus on prime locations.

Location Keys

Summer locations for river pike vary with the nature of the rivers. In smaller rivers, like Colorado's Yampa River, pike hold in the river's deeper holes and below log jams and other debris. These obstructions create breaks from the current, providing prime holding and ambush points. Other location keys include main river points and the inside and outside edges of side-water sloughs. If water levels fall low enough, water temperatures may become too warm in the sloughs, forcing pike to spend more time in the main river. In this case, fish the slowest water you can find that has equal access to deep and shallow water.

Some rivers grow weed beds in summer. I'm not talking about shallow-water vegetation. I'm referring to full-blown cabbage beds that grow toward the surface in ten to twelve feet of water and cover fairly large areas. These beds attract baitfish, and they almost always hold pike. Isolated weed beds located on prime structure, such as a mud flat or saddle, may produce a bonanza.

On large river systems, water levels play a big part in determining the pike's location. Be prepared to cover all possibilities, including the small, interconnected lakes and sloughs and the inside and outside edges of the mouths leading into them. Don't overlook long, shallow flats located around saddles near islands on the main river. When warmer weather dictates, main river points become primary holding areas. Consider what food sources are available, since you'll find pike near them.

During unusually warm periods, pike and other fish seek out cool-water inlets such as springs or creeks. They offer relief during prolonged hot spells, and finding them can spell the difference between success and failure. If you do your homework during the winter months, you may notice open-water pockets that indicate these areas. Make yourself a note or mark their location on a map and come back to them during warm-water periods. You'll increase your success rate twofold!

Daily Movements

The daily movements of pike in rivers are the direct outcome of three factors. The first factor is available food. If the pike's food moves, so must the pike. By knowing the pike's food source, you'll be able to track them and eventually predict where pike will be.

The second factor is water level, which can fluctuate daily. When rivers drop or rise, the pike's daily locations change. It may be gradual, but they will change. If the river is dropping each day, you'll find pike spending more time along the first drop-off in slightly deeper water.

When the river is rising, the pike will likely scatter and stay that way until the level stabilizes.

The third factor is weather. In the northernmost range of the pike, strong, rainy cold fronts can bring daily movements to an abrupt halt. On these river systems, the pike's daily movements are very similar to those in lakes during the post-spawn period—deep to shallow and shallow to deep again, but in summer these movements are likely to occur in the main river, not in the lakes and sloughs. If a severe cold front hits, cover the deeper parts of the main river points and slough mouths I described earlier.

Summer Tactics

River pike fishing requires the use of a boat to be effective day-in and day-out. You need the ability to cover lots of water while fishing rivers, especially in summer. A typical day spent chasing pike in rivers finds me running anywhere from ten to twenty miles of river. To be consistently successful, you have to be mobile, much like the pike you're pursuing.

Start by probing the inside and outside edges of slough and lake mouths where pike hold early. This is best done with a sink-tip fly line and sinking fly. Other areas to prospect include the deep-water drop-offs near islands and main river points. One last location is the drop-offs near shallow mud flats that are typically formed on the downstream side of islands and narrows. All of these areas usually hold pike during the early mornings and late afternoon hours.

When water levels are high enough, water temperatures permit, and food dictates, pike move back into the shallows of the lakes and sloughs, even in the middle of summer. When this happens, it's possible to find conditions similar to the post-spawn period, with large numbers of big fish in shallow water. Fish the backs of these areas with a floating line and a large streamer pattern, such as a Bunny Fly or Deceiver. Of course, it's also possible that the fish you find there will be digesting their last meal and won't be very cooperative. If that happens, focus your efforts more on main river locations where fish might still be actively feeding.

During low-water periods and extremely warm weather, I float and fish the river from the boat. Again I focus on main river points, areas located around the mouths of sloughs and channels, and any deep-water weed beds I can find. Slack, deep-water areas like those downstream of downed trees or rock piles will hold fish, sometimes in numbers under these situations. I vary my presentations between floating lines and streamers and the neutral-density presentation of a full-sink line with a floating, diving-type fly. The neutral-density presentation is deadly on suspended summer pike.

Fall

Now I'm going to shock some people! The fall period in rivers is, without a doubt, my favorite time of year and my favorite place to flyfish for pike. What about the post-spawn period in lakes? Fall flyfishing for pike in rivers can be better. That's right, I said better!

Imagine finding large numbers of big fish in concentrated areas. That sounds like the post-spawn period in lakes, when the location of pike is fairly easy to predict, but there's one noticeable difference that makes river fishing in fall even more exciting. Pike in the fall are bigger. When I say bigger, I don't mean longer. I mean they're carrying more weight. Fall pike weigh as much as twenty to thirty percent more than they

Imagine finding large numbers of big fish in concentrated areas.

did during the post-spawn period. Fall is the pike's last chance to feed freely before winter sets in, and they're aggressive and feeding with purpose. There is little that interrupts them during this glorious time of year in rivers.

Lake pike are also bigger, it's true, but they're spread throughout the lake in fall and not as easy to locate. River pike also have the run of the river in fall, but they have a tendency to concentrate in specific areas, based on water levels, flow, habitat, and available forage.

Let me give you an example of what fall flyfishing for pike in rivers can be like. Six of us entered the mouth of a small side lake that the river spilled into. The weather was chilly with air temperatures in the high forties, and a steady cold rain fell. The river level was normal but rising slowly from the constant rainfall. Not exactly picture-perfect conditions, but you never know how the fishing's going to be until you try it.

Spreading out in groups of two, we began our assault on the lake, which was no bigger than fifty acres. Working the lake from the river mouth toward the back, our group approached the fish much as we would during the post-spawn bite—floating lines rigged with large

The results were great—we could do no wrong.

Bunny-style streamers fished tight to shore as well as over open water. The results were great—we could do no wrong.

The fishing only got better as we approached the back of the lake. Three members of the group lined up parallel to the shoreline about twenty feet apart. Almost every cast resulted in a vicious strike and a heavy fish. The three of us took forty-three fish over forty inches in less than four hours. Seven of those fish measured between forty-seven and fifty inches. The group's total for this one day exceeded 160 fish, with many over the forty-inch mark.

Now you know why I'd rather be on a pike river in the fall!

Water Temperatures

In rivers you can expect to find fall water temperatures falling from the high fifties down into the forties. Since rivers don't stratify, there isn't a fall turnover to worry about. Temperatures are fairly consistent throughout the river system, and you can expect to find fish in many parts of the system. There are some exceptions to this, based on water temperature.

In river systems where there are connecting lakes and large sloughs, you can find isolated areas of warmer water. Increased temperatures come courtesy of solar heating or warm-water sources, such as creeks or springs. You can find spots that might be five to ten degrees warmer than the main river. These areas attract baitfish, and large numbers of hungry pike concentrate there.

Once again, stability is the key to success during the fall. Wild swings in the weather can cause temporary scattering of pike. Pike will be active whether it's hot or cold, but they'll react adversely to big temperature swings and fluctuating water levels, just like they do in other seasons.

Location Keys

With water temperatures in the pike's preferred range, free movement throughout the river system is likely. Finding fall pike in rivers requires that you not only understand water temperatures and their effects but also that you draw upon your knowledge of pike habitat and available prey sources. If you put your knowledge of all three factors to good use, you can experience some of the best pike flyfishing of your life.

That being said, fall location keys are much the same as those in other seasons. High water levels will cause pike to stay near lake and slough mouths. And under the right circumstances, you'll find them in the shallow, weedy flats at the backs of those same lakes and sloughs. With low or falling waters, you'll find the pike concentrated along main river points and the mid-depth mud flats adjacent to them.

Other areas worth your attention are more clearly seen now. Slack-water areas downstream of deadfall and log jams offer cover for pike to hunt and ambush prey. Decaying weed beds also hold some pike, as long as the weeds still have some life left in them. On the Yampa River, the water level is usually low in fall. Pike are forced into the deeper runs located directly below these structures. When this happens, you can eliminate large sections of water and focus on these key spots. Expect to find large numbers of fish holding in these areas, because other popular locations are too shallow or even dry.

Daily Movements

As usual, stability of water level, water temperatures, and the availability of food drive the pike's daily movements. Rising waters allow pike access to areas not available when the water is low; falling waters force pike to retreat to the main river. Water temperatures that are stable or rising slightly during the heat of the day will induce daily movements toward the shallows. Falling temperatures slow or even stop those movements. Daily pike movements then become limited to locations adjacent to main river points, lake and slough mouths, and other key structures located in the main river.

Food is the main driver at this time of year, and it pays to do a little extra homework. By knowing where to find food sources, chances are high you'll find pike. If pike key in to whitefish and the whitefish move into sloughs or lakes, the pike will follow. If perch are on the menu and they move into deep water, the pike will follow.

Let's look at two types of rivers. The first is basically slow-moving, with few side channels, sloughs, or backwater areas. In this type of river, there is little in the way of daily pike movement. Pike concentrate in the slack water located below log jams and downed timber. They also frequent deep pools below slow runs, main river points, and mud flats.

Flies stripped back over deeper water provoked immediate strikes.

The second type of river is one with sloughs and interconnecting lakes. Here you'll see daily movements from deep to shallow and back again. In the morning hours, you'll find pike holding on main points and at the edges of lake and slough mouths. As the day progresses, pike may move toward the shallows, if food is available and water temperatures permit. Evening hours find the pike slowly retreating into the main river.

A story of note is worth telling here. After many successful fall outings to the same river, we thought we'd seen it all and had everything figured out. But one trip found us fishing the usual fall patterns and following the same daily routine, but without our usual success. In the late afternoons, the sloughs and lakes filled up with big fish. The problem was that we were only able to catch a very few of them. It seems most of these fish had full bellies.

After a couple of frustrating days, we stumbled across the answer. While slowly running the main river in our boat, we noticed we were spooking many pike along the bank. Motoring up the bank several hundred yards, we stopped the engine in front of a point where the river cut way back. We slowly drifted about twenty feet from the bank and began casting toward it. Flies stripped back over deeper water provoked immediate strikes. We continued to catch fish until midafternoon, when the action slowly began to dwindle.

Feeling like the cat that ate the canary, we slid back into one of the nearby lakes thinking we might prolong our good fortunes, but our luck stopped there. The pike had keyed in to salmon smolt migrating down the river. The pike were feeding in the main river where food was plentiful, and only when they had a full belly did they slide back into the lakes, where warmer water aided their digestion. If it wasn't for the salmon smolt, in all likelihood the pike would have been content to feed on the whitefish scattered in the lakes. Another lesson learned.

Fall Tactics

With so many variables, it's almost impossible to give you one set of tactics for fall pike in rivers, so I won't even try. Instead, I'll give you several scenarios so you'll be prepared for some of the problems a river in fall might present. By being adaptable, you'll be more successful.

Let's first take a look at a river that has high, rising water levels with cold water temperatures. Under these circumstances, I suggest you just pack your things and go back home. Okay, I'm just kidding, but the fishing will be tough. Begin the day by probing main river points and areas directly outside sloughs and the mouths of connecting lakes, as usual. As the day progresses, venture into the sloughs and lakes and fish the edges where deep water meets the shallows. Cover these waters with sinking lines and weighted flies, because pike hold tight to bottom structure under these conditions. Don't expect lots of movement or very aggressive pike. Slow your presentations, be patient, and cover the water thoroughly.

Next we'll take a look at more favorable conditions: high but stable water levels combined with stable weather. Start your mornings once again along main river points and around lake and slough mouths. Work your way into the lakes or sloughs as the day progresses. By midafternoon you should be working the shallows of the back areas. If this fails to produce pike in numbers and size, return to the main river points and mouth areas. Remember that food will be the key driver, because pike are feeding heavily to carry them through the winter and to prepare them for next spring's spawn.

With high waters that are receding, you'll need to vary your tactics again. If waters have been high for an extended period preceding the drop, pike would have had time to move into the shallow, flooded flats. In this case, your focus should be around the inside and outside edges of the mouths of these flats. Pike will funnel in and out on a daily basis. As water levels continue to fall, pike will spend less time on the flats and more on the outside edges and adjacent main river points. Your presentations won't vary much, with deeper-water pike responding better to sinking lines and large, weighted streamers, while shallow-water pike respond better to floating lines and large Bunny streamers or poppers and divers.

In our next scenario—low-water periods—you should spend most of your time fishing the main river, since the sloughs and side channels will be too low to hold any big fish. They may even dry up completely under extreme conditions. So, start your day as always by probing main river points and saddles between islands. Be prepared to fish slightly deeper water earlier in the mornings using sinking lines and weighted streamers with short leaders to keep your flies close to the bottom.

You should move toward shallower waters in the afternoon. By this I mean you should fish tighter to shorelines and structure. Start with the main river points and saddles, but also check where lakes or sloughs drain into the main river. Other areas worth exploring are shallow and mid-depth mud flats located around islands. The best afternoon tactics include using floating lines and large, Bunny-style streamers in these areas. When fishing isolated mud flats, make sure to cover them completely, even into slightly deeper water directly above and below them.

In the next scenario, low water levels that are quickly on the rise cause pike to scatter. This might be the toughest condition you face in rivers, since rapidly rising water offers pike new territory to explore daily. In this cases, you'll be called on to use all you've learned about river pike throughout the season.

Under these conditions, focus on main river points and mid-river flats until water levels begin to stabilize. Once that happens, leave those areas and explore lake and slough mouths, particularly along their outside edges. When water levels permit, begin to explore the backs of lakes and sloughs. Be prepared with sinking and floating lines and a wide range of fly patterns, as you'll likely face many different situations.

———————

We know that rivers are ever-changing bodies of water. Daily changes can come in the form of run-off, heavy rains, and releases from dams. Tributaries can cause wild fluctuations in water levels, water clarity, and speed of flow. All of these things contribute to the seasonal and daily movements of pike within them, and it's a constant challenge to know how these events will affect where pike hold.

As the seasons change and the river with them, your tactics and presentations must change, too. I've given you many scenarios and many options with which to approach them. Be flexible in your approach, understand the effects of water levels on pike location, and you'll be well on your way to becoming successful in your pursuit of river pike. I think you'll agree that rivers have much to offer the pike enthusiast by extending the season and offering some relatively untouched flyfishing for really big pike.

North American Pike Rivers

This section is meant to provide a representative sampling to lead you to some of the more productive pike rivers. It's not an exhaustive list by any means.

By the way, all the rivers here have already been discovered and written about in the angling press. Lesser-known rivers often produce better fishing than that found in more well-known rivers. I know several excellent rivers whose names have yet to be seen in print, and for that reason, I hope you'll understand if I don't mention them. You may fish a river that you know produces well. Chances are I've probably fished it, too, and wish to keep it from being widely known as long as possible. Those places are getting harder and harder to find and even more difficult to keep secret. Rest assured, the secret's safe with me.

Alaska: Yukon River and its tributaries, including Innoko River, Iditarod River, Minto Flats, Kaiyuh Flats, Susitna River, Tanana River, Kuskokwim River

Rivers offer relatively untouched flyfishing for really big pike.

Canada: Red River, Winnipeg River, Churchill River, William River,
  Saskatchewan River (just to name a few)
Connecticut: Connecticut River
Colorado: Yampa River, Rio Grande River
Illinois: Mississippi River, Des Plaines River, Kankakee River, trib-
  utaries of Lake Michigan
Indiana: Yellow River
Iowa: Upper Mississippi River
Maryland: Potomac River and some of its tributaries, Youghighany
  River, Conococheague Creek
Massachusetts: Connecticut River, Charles River
Michigan: tributaries of Lake Michigan
Minnesota: Mississippi River, Rainy River, Warroad River, Winter
  Road River, Red River, Baudette River (just to name a few)
Montana: Upper Flathead River
New Mexico: Rio Grande River
New York: St. Lawrence River, Raquette River, Seneca River
North Dakota: Missouri River, Red River, Yellowstone River
Ohio: tributaries of Lake Erie
Pennsylvania: Ohio River, Allegheny River, and their tributaries
South Dakota: Big Sioux River, Missouri River
West Virginia: Ohio River
Wisconsin: Mississippi River, lower sections of the Wisconsin River

Once again, this is just a short list of rivers that offer pike action. I hope
this gives you an idea of just how many rivers are available to the pike
enthusiast. I strongly urge you to contact local wildlife offices before
you plan a trip to any of these areas. With their help, you may discover
other nearby waters that provide additional opportunities to pursue
river pike on the fly.

FIVE

Presentations for Pike on the Fly

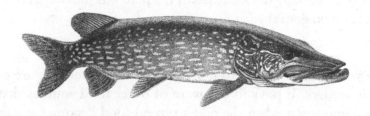

Question: What does a pike eat?
Answer: Anything it wants!

I experienced this firsthand when a fellow angler landed a pike at a local lake. Noticing a rather odd, disc-shaped object bulging near the pike's belly, we decided to dissect the pike and examine what it had eaten. We discovered three eight-inch suckers and, to our surprise, one small turtle.

While I'm not going give you the recipe for a turtle fly and presentation tactics to fish it, this story does illustrate my point. A pike will eat most anything—or at least attempt to—if it can get its mouth around it. These menu items include, but are not limited to, other fish, crayfish, birds, small mammals, and even the occasional turtle, as we found out. Pike have also been observed gorging themselves on a variety of smaller things, including leeches, damselfly nymphs, and even scuds. It's just another example of why pike are so successful—they're adaptable!

Northern pike can routinely eat things roughly one-third their own size. A thirty-inch pike can eat a ten-inch fish with no problem, but pike have been known to attempt much larger meals. More than once, I've found a pike that had choked to death trying to eat too large a fish. The most striking example was the thirty-eight-inch pike I mentioned in an earlier chapter that choked on a twenty-inch largemouth bass.

In over twenty years of pursuing pike, I've witnessed pike attacking muskrats, mice, and lemmings. While eating lunch on a bluff overlooking a lake, I watched a mother duck and four ducklings make their merry way across a bay. Then I noticed an ominous shadow several feet directly beneath the ducks. Sensing the danger, the mother duck became frantic, flapping her wings and quacking hysterically. About this time the water erupted, and all hell broke loose. As the water calmed and the scattered ducks regrouped, I counted them. One momma duck and one, two, three baby ducks! It seems the pike was playing a cruel game of duck, duck, goose!

———————

I give you these examples to illustrate the point that pike are opportunistic feeders. It pays to be aware of other food sources that may become important when the pike's typical food becomes scarce. The patterns you'll be fishing day-in and day-out, however, are ones that mimic baitfish, which are always in the pike's diet. In most lakes, small fish are the most readily available and most abundant food source.

Pike prefer soft-ray fish, such as trout, suckers, and whitefish, over spiny-ray fish, such as perch and walleye. Knowing these preferences and what species are available in a lake or river will enable you to "match the hatch" pike-style by using a streamer that comes closest to the size, shape, and color of the prey fish.

In this chapter, I'll discuss the general fly patterns that have been most effective for me over the years. Additionally, I'll briefly describe the circumstances in which I find them most effective. Most of this chapter is devoted to an in-depth discussion of the ways I fish each type of pattern. First I'll cover streamers, including attractor and realistic patterns, both weighted and unweighted. For those who favor top-water action, I'll discuss divers and poppers and cover some unusual ways to present them that will help trigger strikes from persnickety pike.

Pike's Moods Revisited

Before I start on presentations, I want to remind you about the pike's moods. Remember that pike have three distinct moods—positive, neutral, and negative. You can determine their mood by observing how they behave and how they react to your presentations. Learning to read these moods will help you determine the best flies and retrieves to use to trigger a response.

Luckily, pike are usually fairly easy to spot, allowing you to judge their mood. In cases where poor visibility prevents you from seeing the pike, you'll need to rely on what you've learned from the times you have been able to see them. I'll give you some pointers on spotting pike later in this chapter.

The time of year, weather, and water levels also offer clues to the pike's moods. When sight fishing is not possible, pay special attention to the speed of your retrieve when pike hit your fly. High-speed retrieves that provoke a response signal positive, aggressive pike, while slower retrieves that trigger strikes usually signal pike in a more neutral mood. Obviously, little or no response to your presentations signals a negative mood.

Positive pike really require no special consideration or presentation. They are very active and easily caught. Stable conditions surround pike at this time, and with everything right in the pike's world, there is little you can do wrong. Top-water flies, divers, and streamers fished near the surface, at mid-depths, and on the bottom will all produce. These are glorious days that you'll relive over and over, particularly when fishing gets tougher. Enjoy them because they don't come along often.

These are glorious days that you'll relive over and over, particularly when fishing gets tougher.

Neutral pike require a little more thought and effort. This mood is signaled by pike that lazily follow your fly, raising your hopes and your heart rate before slowly disappearing into the depths. These pike require you to dig into your bag of tricks. First, change your retrieve, trying all the retrieves I'll describe in this chapter. Second, change your fly. Change the size first, then the color, and finally the shape. At each change of fly, try all the retrieves again.

Negative pike are the ones that cause anglers with a full head of hair to go bald in a matter of minutes. On more than one occasion, my frustration has made me want to turn my fly rod into a javelin and throw it at distances that would win me a medal in the summer Olympics. These pike have shut down due to extreme water temperatures or water-level fluctuations. While they're next to impossible to catch, a negative fish can occasionally be provoked into a strike using an ultra-slow presentation kept close to the bottom.

When you find pike in this frame of mind and there are other fishing options, take advantage of them. If you're 2,000 miles from home with no other option, read on and pay close attention to my presentation using a full-sink line and weighted streamer. It can help save an otherwise lost trip.

Keep in mind that the duration of these moods depends on Mother Nature's clock, and it's likely you'll see pike exhibit several moods in a day's fishing. Knowing how to identify these moods and determining which presentations to use will ensure you the best opportunity for at least some action throughout the day.

Streamers

Streamer patterns are designed to imitate baitfish and other foods, such as crayfish and leeches. I estimate that eighty percent of my pike fishing is done with streamers! Why? It's simple. More times than not, pike are feeding on other fish. As I've said, they're the most available, most abundant prey.

Realistic streamer patterns closely imitate the size, color, and silhouette of the fish pike are feeding on, but some streamers can also represent other food items. A black Bunny Fly, for example, can mimic many kinds of prey, including a small, fleeing baitfish or a large, free-swimming leech. It will even be taken for a crayfish when fished tight to the bottom.

While streamers such as Bunny Flies can imitate many things, pike usually take them as a specific food item. In Colorado, large pike experience extremely heavy angling pressure. Learning the prey they're after and fishing a fly that matches it closely can mean the difference between success and failure. These pike grow to large sizes because they're selective about what they eat. For instance, when the pike are keyed in to stocker trout, your fly should be close in size, color, and shape to a small trout and should mimic the action of the real thing.

Trout flyfishermen are used to matching their flies to the insects on which trout are feeding. But pike fishermen often don't take the time or don't realize they need to figure out what pike are eating and then try to match it. When pike are heavily fished over and when they're larger and more experienced, choosing a fly that imitates what they're eating will make a huge difference.

Elevenmile Reservoir in Colorado offers flyfishers the chance to test their pike angling skills against some of the smartest and largest pike in the state. While working one of the reservoir's small back bays many years ago, I noticed several large pike slowly working along the weed-choked bottom. Occasionally the pike would stop and stick their snouts deep into the vegetation in a probing manner. Every so often a pike would quickly bolt after prey it had spooked. Obviously these pike were hunting for something specific, and when they found it, they quickly pounced on it.

Armed with my usual Bunny Fly, I quickly began casting to these aggressively feeding pike. My first cast failed to capture any interest, as did the following twenty or so. Being the eternal optimist, I simply switched colors from white to black and began casting over the pike once more. The results were the same—no takers! I was starting to get frustrated. In fact, I was real frustrated. I cast once more, placed the rod under my arm, and began fumbling through my fly box, looking for a solution. That's when things started to get interesting.

While I was pondering my fly box, my fly sunk down into the weed bed. By the time I'd picked a new pattern, the fly had become firmly

A black Bunny Fly can mimic many kinds of prey, including a small baitfish or a large leech.

tangled in the weeds, and I had to give the line a quick jerk to free the fly. As the fly cleared the vegetation tight to the bottom, it prompted an abrupt strike from a large pike. My reel screamed as the pike made a mad dash through the weedy forest in which it was feeding. The surface of the lake was soon littered with weeds that had been sliced by the fly line hauled along by the departing pike.

Several tense moments later, the pike neared my reach. Looking down at the spent pike, I admired what appeared to be a decent fish. Nice, I thought, but nowhere near the size of several of the other pike I'd seen working the area. Did I ever tell you that judging the size of pike in the water can be misleading at best? I reached down and tried to snake grab the pike, but I quickly found that I couldn't even get my open hand across its back. As I backed up toward shallower water, I began to realize just how big she was.

Sliding my free hand under her belly to work down toward the tail, I noticed she was full of what felt like rocks. It wasn't rocks in her belly, it was crayfish, and lots of them. These pike had keyed in to the abundance of crayfish and were playing cat and mouse with them in the weeds where the crayfish tried to hide from the hungry pike.

In this case, the problem wasn't that I was using a fly the pike wouldn't eat because of the way it looked. The Bunny Fly can imitate a crayfish just fine. It was my presentation. I simply needed to get the fly down to where the pike were feeding and make it act like a scared crayfish. And that's why I'll spend lots of time in this chapter talking about presentation, as well as patterns.

The rest of that afternoon found me casting and counting down as my fly sank. As I probed the weedlines, I caught a total of four pike. The smallest was forty-four inches. So how big was the first one? That fish was so big around—almost twenty-three inches—that it made its overall length of forty-seven inches seem short! By the way, that fish nudged the thirty-pound mark and is my largest pike to date here in Colorado! For those of you wondering where that bay is, I'm not going to tell you, because I still fish it today, as I watch people pass it by. Guess they're the ones who haven't read my books.

There are two points I'd like to make with this story. First is the fact that generic streamers such as Bunny Flies can imitate anything and everything, from fish to crayfish, providing you match the size, shape, color, and action of the natural. Second is the importance of the manner in which you present the fly. As I've just shown, swimming the fly produced no action in this situation, while a slow "fall-down" and quick, short retrieve through the weeds mimicked the fleeing crayfish being pursued by the evil-eyed marauders.

Streamer Types

I like to break streamers into two basic categories, realistic and attractor. Realistic patterns closely resemble in size, shape, and color the natural forage on which the pike are feeding. Attractor patterns are usually bright, gaudy-colored flies, occasionally adorned with ample amounts of flash to attract the pike and provoke a strike. I break streamers down further into weighted and unweighted versions that I use to cover the water column from top to bottom.

Knowledge of the food sources available is obviously important in selecting the most effective fly. The other part of the formula has to do with the pike's mood—its reaction to your offerings. These two factors together dictate what patterns you should fish and how you should present them.

You don't hear trout fishermen talking about the "mood" of trout very often, but as I've tried to emphasize, it's something a pike flyfisher soon finds to be a very important thing to understand. Paying attention to the pike's mood leads to an understanding of the what, when, and where of streamer fishing for pike.

Realistic Streamers

One of the most realistic patterns is the D's Minnow. This fly can be tied to mimic the size, shape, and color of specific forage fish by simply changing its components. The recipe for this fly and others I'll mention in this chapter can be found in the next chapter.

I cannot overstate the importance of knowing the forage base of the waters you'll be fishing. Doing your homework will pay off. Get on the phone and make some calls to guides, wildlife officials, shops, and lodges in the area you'll be fishing to see what the forage base of the lake or river is. Don't show up at a lake with a perch-colored D's Minnow tied the size of a small minnow and expect the pike to react favorably when their main forage is twelve-inch rainbow trout!

In realistic patterns, you must match the size of the forage fish, as well as their coloration. Keep your offerings proportional to the natural. On one of my local lakes where spottail shiners are numerous and provide easy pickings, I do well throwing a small (#1/0), gray-and-white D's Minnow when the fish there are keyed in to them. Later in the season, the pike shift their attention to stocker trout that run eight to ten inches. Then I switch to a #3/0 or #4/0 D's Minnow that's colored to match. Fishing either pattern during the wrong period may produce the occasional fish, but fishing the spottail pattern when they're the prevalent forage or the rainbow pattern when they are on the pike's menu produces far better results.

The overall shape of the fly is important, as well. In lakes where bluegill are the prey base, a "taller" profile will be necessary to imitate the build of a bluegill. You can match the size and the color fairly easily, but without the shape of a bluegill, your offering will be lacking a key component that might make the difference between success and failure. Don't cheat yourself by tying a pattern in bluegill colors that's shaped like a minnow. Instead, try a broad-bodied pattern, such as a Roger's Big-Eye Baitfish tied in the Hot Tamale version, to offer a realistic bluegill profile and color scheme.

The final key to realistic imitations is action. How does the fly act in the water? Does it come alive or is it stiff and rigid? Some materials naturally come alive in the water. Rabbit fur, marabou, and feathers all spring to life in the water, and flies tied with them require very little action from the angler to make them seem alive.

The problem with natural materials is that they soak up an enormous amount of water, making them heavy and difficult to cast. Synthetics, on the other hand, shed water and are generally lightweight. The trade-off here is that most of the synthetic materials lack natural action and require the fly designer or the angler to create ways to impart action. With its diving collar, the Dahlberg Megadiver creates action in its synthetic tail with the turbulence and rippling effect created by the collar as the fly is pulled through the water. Another way to create action in stiff synthetic materials is to use vigorous strips as the fly is retrieved.

The stop-and-go retrieve described later in this chapter also helps create action in the fly, but it's not always the best retrieve to use, particularly when pike are looking for aggressive retrieves.

Some of the more successful realistic streamers include the D's Minnow, Lefty's Big Fish Deceiver, Roger's Big-Eye Baitfish, Kintz's Bunker Fly, Emmons' Yak Fly, and my favorite staple, the Bunny Fly. The color in all these patterns can be changed to match the natural forage base. That, along with the fact that each of these patterns offers a slightly different combination of size, shape, and action, gives you the ability to match the hatch pike-style.

Attractor Streamers

While they might suggest a baitfish in size and shape, attractor streamers have color schemes that imitate nothing in the pike's natural environment. Instead they're designed to provoke a response with their bright, flashy colors. Color schemes run the gamut. They can have two tones—red/white, yellow/red, or chartreuse/hot orange—or even more combinations. Whatever the color, they're meant to visually stimulate a response.

When the water is the color of a bad cup of coffee, a generous amount of flash added to attractor streamers makes them more visible. The liberal use of materials such as Flashabou and Krystal Flash can greatly improve the effectiveness of attractor patterns in dirty water. In determining how much flash to use, my approach is this—it's easier to cut out materials than it is to add them after the fly has been tied! I always tie in a little more flash than I think it needs, with the intention of trimming the excess as water conditions dictate.

My favorite attractor patterns include two-toned Bunny Flies, Flashtail Whistlers, and Barry's Woolhead Pike Fly. I also do well with Roger's Big-Eye Baitfish (Hot Tamale version) and Bunnyceivers. Do I really need all these patterns? In a word—yes! Each of these flies offers a different size, shape, and action to suggest various forage fish. For instance, Bunny Flies suggest a longer, more cylindrical fish in size and shape, while Roger's Big-Eye Baitfish offers a shorter, bulkier profile. Remember that the keys to good streamer design include size and shape.

Weighted Streamers

Although they're not my favorite choice, weighted streamers have earned their place among my top flies. Most standard pike streamers can be converted to sinking, jig-style flies by adding weighted cones, beads, or dumbbell eyes. Weighted versions give you the ability to reach pike that are holding or feeding tight to bottom structure in deep water. These patterns excel when pike are in a neutral to negative mood and are not actively feeding. These times call for slow and deliberate presentations.

My favorites include Clouser's Half-and-Half, Popovic's Jiggy Fly and Deep Candy, and lead-eyed versions of Flashtail Whistlers and Burk's Hot Claw Crayfish. I fish these patterns in combination with floating lines and varying leader lengths to get a true jigging effect over shallow to mid-depth water. When I want to use the jigging effect near the bottom, I switch to a sink-tip line and short leader. To get on the bottom and stay there, a full-sink line does the trick. I'll discuss presentations for weighted streamers later in this section.

Streamer Tactics

Whether you're using realistic patterns or attractors, weighted or unweighted, you must think like a fish—the fish you're imitating! How would the fish swim, where would it swim, and how would it react when pursued by a large, hungry pike?

The single biggest mistake I've seen flyfishers make has to do with how a baitfish reacts when chased, and it happens when a big pike pursues their fly. They slow down their retrieves, as though trying to allow the pike to catch up to the fly. Trust me, pike will catch up to your fly without your help! Think of it this way, if you were a baitfish being chased by the jaws of death, would you slow down or put on your track shoes and get the hell out of there?

I choose tactics that work, based on the time of year, the weather conditions, and what the pike are feeding on. Knowing how a particular forage fish swims through the water allows me to use the right retrieve. Knowing where they live allows me to present my fly at the proper depth. While clear water tells me to present flies with natural, imitative colors and dirty water requires bold, flashy attractor patterns, the mood of the pike plays a part in all of it and forces me to change

If you were a baitfish being chased by the jaws of death, would you slow down or put on your track shoes and get the hell out of there?

my fly, my presentation, or both. After making those adjustments, I can decide whether I need to start pulling my hair out.

Before I get into the retrieves, a quick discussion of the angles of presentation is in order. At the water's edge, I like to fan cast through the area before wading out. This gives me a chance to catch fish I might spook if I just waded into the water.

Once I've waded out, I position myself to move parallel to the shoreline. I break down the water in front of me into five sections, and I'll start with one cast in each section. The first cast is in a direct line between me and the shoreline. The next cast is at an angle between me and the shoreline, toward the direction I'm wading. The third cast is directly in front. The fourth cast is toward deeper water at an angle away from the shore, and the final cast is in a direct line away from shore.

At the beginning of this book, I talked about the pike's eyesight and the fact that presentations made at angles to the lie of the fish keep the fly in the pike's line of sight longer. It also presents the fly to them more naturally. By dividing the water up in this manner, I not only

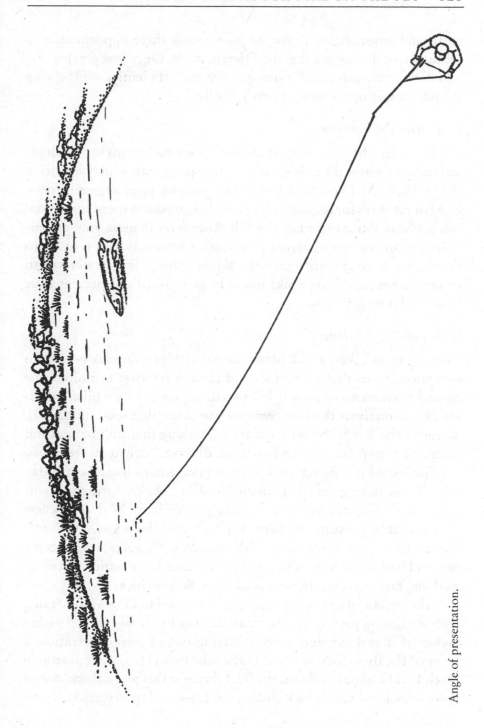

Angle of presentation.

create and cover angles, I give the pike two or three opportunities to see the fly, each time at a slightly different angle. Once you get this system down, you can cover water quickly and efficiently, while giving the pike ample opportunity to eat your fly.

Basic Straight Retrieve

The basic straight retrieve involves four- to six-inch strips in a methodical fashion, where the only variable is the speed with which you bring the fly back. As I've said, I like to rate pike by their aggressiveness. Use fast retrieves for aggressive, positive fish, medium speed for neutral fish, and slow retrieves for negative fish. Always try to make your presentations at angles by quartering your casts. Obviously, this is easier to do when you're able to sight-fish. When fishing dirty water, try to imagine where and how a pike might be positioned and present your fly at angles to that spot.

Stop-and-Go Retrieve

Every now and then we all break the rules! Flyfishing for pike is no exception. Even though you should always try first to imitate the natural movements of prey fish—a baitfish pursued by a pike, for instance—sometimes the best retrieves are those that seem unnatural. When all else has failed, why not try something that isn't natural and shouldn't work? The stop-and-go is one of those "unnatural" retrieves.

I discovered just how right the wrong presentation can be one day when I was fishing ice-out pike on Nejalini Lake in northern Manitoba. Late ice limited access to the lake's many bays. With only a few bays available, pressure on them was high, and the pike ... well, let's just say they got suspicious of all the standard offerings. I tried every pattern I had in different colors and sizes. I used basic retrieves at slow, medium, fast, and even hyper-speed rates. Still no luck.

In the middle of one of my retrieves, I stopped to discuss something with my fishing partner. A pike following my fly slowly slid up within inches of it and stopped as well. Acting out of pure frustration, I stripped the fly as hard as I could. The pike bolted from a dead stop to Mach 1 and instantly inhaled the fly. I thought this was a fluke, one of those occasional dumb-luck strikes, but I cast and tried it again. Three strips of the line and a pause. Three hard strips of the line and wham! Another fish on. Soon my partner was on to this stop-and-go retrieve and quickly into a fish as well.

Ever heard the saying, curiosity killed the cat? I believe the stop-and-go retrieve triggers that type of response. The pike don't really want to eat the fly, but they just can't help themselves. I'm not sure whether that's actually true, but this retrieve can make pike pounce like a kitten on a ball of yarn. After a slow start to that day, we finished with forty-three pike that fell for the stop-and-go retrieve. This technique has saved many other frustrating days.

Variable-Speed Retrieve

The variable-speed retrieve is a teasing retrieve that works very well when used in conjunction with streamers that breathe in the water. It works exceedingly well with Bunny Flies, as the fur undulates through the water as the retrieve changes speed. It teases the pike by slowly and tantalizingly moving the fly in front of them and then quickly zipping it away. It creates the illusion of an alarmed baitfish that's just discovered it's in dangerous territory. This is a great trick for provoking pike that are on the edge between neutral and positive. It has a tendency to push them over the edge.

I also like to use this retrieve when I'm fishing new water or if conditions have changed, causing a swing in the pike's mood. By varying the speed, casting at angles, and paying attention to when the strike occurs, I can determine the speed the pike react to best. While this a great search tool, it's also a terrific presentation that can stand on its own merits.

The difference between the stop-and-go retrieve and the variable-speed approach is simple—I never stop the retrieve. Instead I'll make one long, slow strip followed by several short, quick strips. I sometimes reverse the process by starting with several short, quick strips followed by one long, slow strip. I build off this process by varying the speed and length of the strips. Use your imagination with this retrieve.

Change-in-Direction Retrieve

When a straight retrieve or even the stop-and-go method fails to produce, I have one last "trick retrieve" up my sleeve. Fleeing baitfish rarely

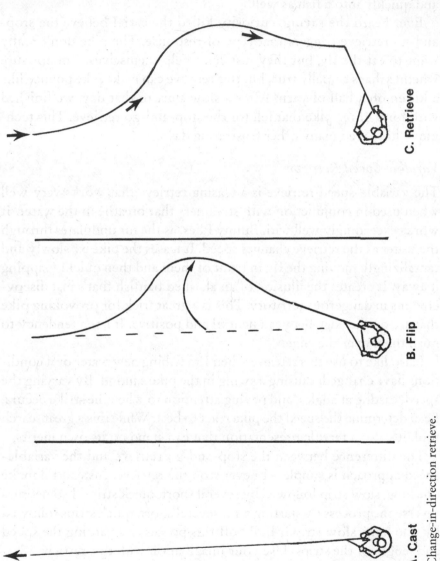

C. Retrieve

B. Flip

A. Cast

Change-in-direction retrieve.

swim in a straight line when something is trying to eat them. Instead, their speeds and movements are erratic, to say the least. We can use the stop-and-go method to mimic their unpredictable swimming speed, but what about their movements? Try my change-in-direction retrieve!

It was through observation that this idea was born. I was sitting on the front end of a boat during some slow fishing when I got my first glimpse of what terrifying horror a fish goes through when it's pursued by a pike. No fewer than six good-sized suckers went flying by the boat in a frantic attempt to escape being eaten. I was certain it had to be a pike chasing these fish, but the water grew calm as quickly as it had erupted, with no sign of the perpetrator.

Scanning the water, I found the culprit on the other side of the boat. A forty-inch pike had taken up a position in three feet of water on the shore side of the boat. Fighting the urge to cast to it, I sat still and watched. The pike's fins and tail quivered in anticipation of its next meal. Slowly the pike drifted toward shore.

Then, in a flash, the pike was in pursuit again. The suckers had unwittingly swum back toward it. The pike was clearly not swimming at full speed. It seemed to be moving in a calculated way, almost as though it was measuring the suckers for the kill or waiting for one to make a fatal mistake.

I made two important observations. The first was that the pike was pushing or herding these fish toward an obstruction, in this case the shore, where they'd have to turn, providing the pike a better angle of attack. The second observation was how a fish reacts when being pursued. Erratic would be the best term to describe the way those suckers swam in their attempt to escape. They made numerous, quick changes in direction.

The two key words here are angle and erratic. I've already talked about presenting your fly at angles to pike, and now I've given an example of the prey's erratic swimming behavior. Don't you want to mimic these factors in your presentation?

The change-in-direction retrieve can be achieved by first casting about thirty feet of line. During the retrieve, roll cast the back half of the line to the left or right. By doing this, your fly will change direction about midway on its way back. If the direction change doesn't provoke a strike, I'll roll cast another bend in the line, this time in the opposite direction. I can usually get in two or three changes of direction during a retrieve.

The change of direction in mid-retrieve seems to really irritate pike and often provokes a violent response immediately. I lovingly refer to it as "flushing the toilet," because there's a big void where the fly once was, followed by a slow, giant swirl that looks like it might lead to the bottom of the lake.

Covering the Water Column

You must be prepared to cover the water top to bottom, from the shallows to as much as twelve to fifteen feet deep. Pike feed throughout the water column in all seasons, as water temperatures and food sources dictate. This means you must know and use all the streamer presentation options I'll discuss in this section, if you want to catch pike in almost any situation.

The depths at which pike feed can be divided into four categories: surface, subsurface, suspended, and bottom. With different line, leader, and fly combinations, you can make presentations at each depth.

By using creative combinations of fly lines, and streamer types and weights, you can make vertical, horizontal, and suspended (neutral-density) presentations, many of which will be new to most pike. Some of these presentations allow you to fish the fly to the pike in a natural way, while others are so distinctly different that they use the pike's curiosity to attract it.

Don't try to fish the same way in ten feet of water as you do in three. You won't be successful consistently. I have a saying, "If you can't get the pike to come to the fly, then take the fly to the pike."

If the water is ten feet deep but pike are feeding over the tops of weed beds near the surface, you can effectively fish an unweighted streamer near the surface with a floating line. If pike are feeding among those same weed beds, you can fish in open-water pockets or the inside and outside edges of the beds with a sink-tip line and a diving fly. This neutral-density presentation allows you to fish deeper in the column of water. It has been my number-one producer for suspended pike and tiger muskies, at home in Colorado and fishing abroad.

There's a big void where the fly once was, followed by a slow, giant swirl that looks like it might lead to the bottom of the lake—"flushing the toilet."

Summer heat or choice of prey can force pike to feed tight to bottom structure and cover in water ten feet deep. In this situation, a full-sink line may be necessary to take your fly down to where pike are feeding. Be flexible, be adaptable, and you'll ultimately be successful!

Floating Line/Unweighted Streamer

With a floating line and an unweighted streamer, I can create the illusion of a free-swimming forage fish ripe for the taking. This is an excellent choice for shallow water when pike are aggressively pursuing food. Leader lengths run between six and eight feet, mostly dependent upon water clarity and how spooky the pike are. The more aggressive the pike are, the shorter your leader can be.

This setup also works well for fishing over and around the tops of submerged weed beds, when pike are holding in them. Pike are on constant lookout from below for unsuspecting food. When weeds push toward the surface and the pike are feeding in the upper part of the water column, make sure you fish into the open pockets, over the tops of the weeds, and along the outside edges of the weed beds using this setup.

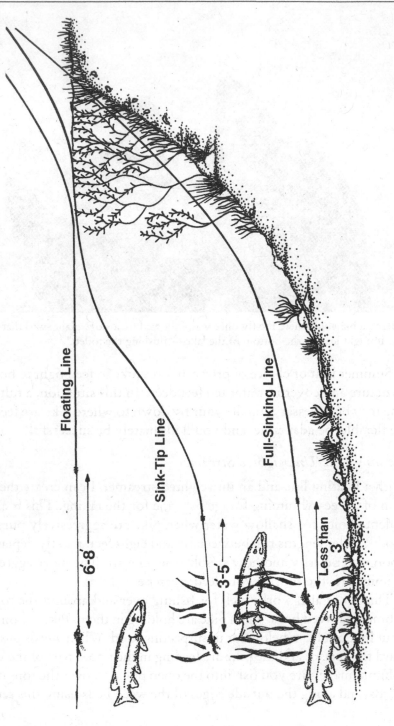

Floating Line

Sink-Tip Line

Full-Sinking Line

6-8′

3-5′

Less than 3′

Unweighted streamer presentation.

Sink-Tip Line/Unweighted Streamer

Another setup I like to fish is a sink-tip line in conjunction with a short, three- to five-foot leader and an unweighted streamer. With this combination, you can give the illusion of a fish making a break for the surface from deeper water. It's an excellent choice for midsummer pike when they're hunkered down in the weed beds or during the post-spawn bite before pike have made their way into shallow, warming waters in the afternoons.

Full-Sink Line/Unweighted Streamer

My least favorite way to fish unweighted streamers, but a highly effective method nonetheless, is to use a high-density, full-sink line. Using these lines with an unweighted streamer and a very short leader (about thirty inches) allows you to present the fly tight to the bottom when pike are feeding there on prey such as suckers or leeches.

This presentation requires patience while you wait for both the line and the fly to reach the desired depth. It works well when strong weather patterns force pike to retreat to deeper water. In these situations, pike will not be willing to move far, so slow retrieves are the norm.

Weighted-Streamer Presentations

By weighting streamers, you open up a new realm of possibilities, allowing you to make vertical presentations to the pike. Then, by using different line types, you can change the angles at which you present the flies. As I begin to describe the possibilities, I think you'll agree that flyfishing for pike is anything but two-dimensional.

In the world of conventional angling, fishing with jigs is considered one of the most effective ways to take all species of fish, including pike. This flyfisher has learned that we can mimic the fish-catching characteristics of the jig almost as well as we've learned to imitate what fish eat. As flyfishermen continue to expand their interests to include other species of fish, they need to borrow presentations from conventional angling and modify them to work with the flyfishing tools available today.

Floating Line/Weighted Streamer

One of the most productive ways to catch pike on fly tackle incorporates the use of a floating line and a weighted streamer with a long leader (nine feet). I call it the float/sink presentation. Most people find this combination odd; I find it deadly. Many anglers look puzzled when I describe using a Clouser's Half-and-Half on a floating line over deeper water. One gentleman even asked if I knew what the hell I was doing. As I explained to him, when wade fishing in shallow water and fishing over deeper water where pike are holding tight to bottom structure, this technique is excellent.

When I want to imitate a "jigging" action with a fly, this combination works best, because it allows for great vertical coverage of the water column. A sinking line and weighted fly combination creates a similar effect, but the vertical water coverage is reduced dramatically because the sinking line keeps the fly tighter to the bottom. The sink/sink combination has its place, but I'll get to that a little later.

After casting over deep water, allow the fly to sink to the bottom. (Here's a tip: many strikes occur during the fall of the fly.) Assuming the water you're fishing is about eight to nine feet in depth, double the depth to get your countdown. In this case, do a sixteen- to eighteen-second count, giving the fly time to reach the bottom.

At this point, begin your retrieve. Two sharp strips of the floating line make the fly clear the bottom and rise several feet. Now, pause and allow the fly to fall again. Of course, as the fly moves into shallower water, your retrieves and down counts get shorter. This takes some practice and getting used to, but I guarantee results, especially for less-than-receptive pike in a neutral to negative mood. It's especially effective when pike are holding tight to bottom structure in slightly deeper water after a cold front has pushed through. Remember to keep your presentations slow and allow time for the fly to sink between strips. Be patient. The rewards can be great.

It's very important to maintain contact with the fly through your touch on the line. And keep a keen eye on the line, as the only signal of a take may be a slight twitch in the end of your fly line. When that happens, slowly tighten the line until you feel weight on the other end, set the hook, and hang on.

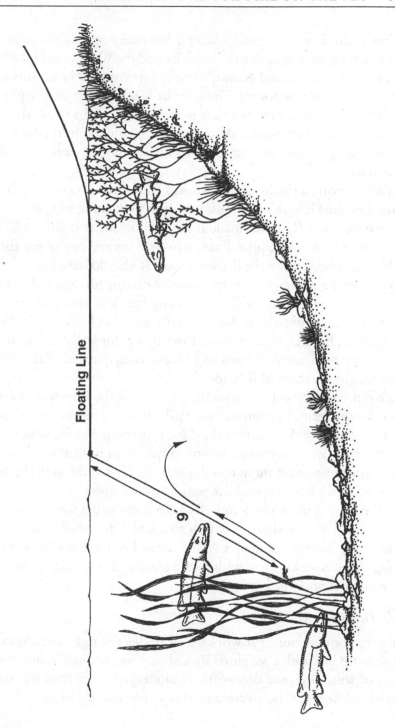

Weighted streamer presentation: Floating line.

This technique has served me well for many sport fish—peacock bass in Brazil, smallmouth bass in the Boundary Waters, and pike from Colorado to Canada and Alaska. On my last trip to Alaska, this technique got a regular workout. The pike had slid into seven to eight feet of water and refused every other presentation, even those that had worked before they moved. After I finally switched to the float/sink presentation, a so-so day turned into a you-should-have-been-there kind of day.

Wading along a shallow mud point, I found the drop-off to deeper water. I probed it with my Clouser. It didn't take long to hook up. On the first cast, my fly never made it to the bottom as it fell, and I was immediately into a nice pike. Ever curious, I invited one of my fishing buddies to wade out on the flat with me. He should have known there was a catch. I encouraged him to continue casting his Bunny Fly in the same area I was fishing the Clouser using the float-sink presentation. After four hours of fishing, the final tally stood at Clouser 32, Bunny Fly 1. Now, before you complain, I'm not a completely inconsiderate person. We did trade rods back and forth, so my partner in the experiment caught his share of fish, too!

We did try different line combinations with the Bunny and even a few other patterns, but almost every pike that afternoon was taken on the fall of the fly. Sometimes they took it immediately, other times halfway back in the retrieve, and still other times right at our feet. The single most important thing was the way the fly fell through the water column. That's what tripped the pike's strike response.

If I'm fishing from a boat or belly boat and casting toward the shallow water along the shore, I switch to a sink-tip or full-sink line. Instead of the bottom rising up toward me as I retrieve my fly, it will be giving away. A sinking line with a short leader is necessary to keep the fly in contact with the bottom.

Sink-Tip/Weighted Streamer

Another combination that works well under the right circumstances is a sink-tip line with a weighted fly fished along the inside and outside edges of weed beds and drop-offs. A moderately weighted fly such as a Flashtail Whistler is effective in this combination, because it sinks

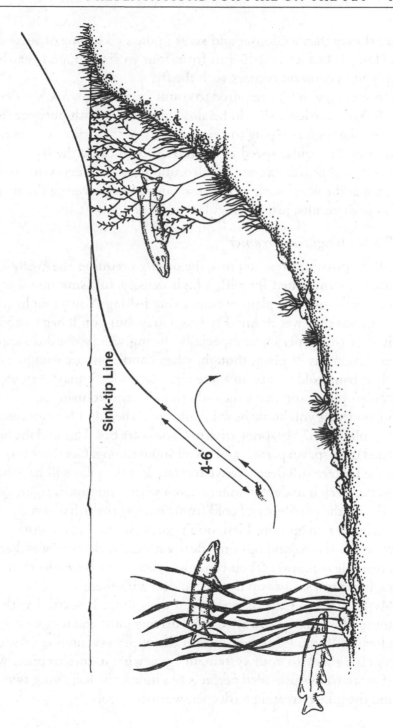

Weighted streamer presentation: Sink-tip line.

more slowly than a Clouser and stays in the strike zone of suspended pike longer. Leader lengths run from four to six feet, and that helps keep you in constant contact with the fly.

Once again you'll be required to count your fly down to the desired depth. Your retrieves should be slow but steady, with purpose. Keep in mind that you're trying to keep your fly in the strike zone as much as possible. Irregular speed in the retrieve will cause the fly to fall or rise out of the strike zone. It's also important to keep your rod tip pointed at the water surface, because raising and lowering the tip produces poor results, just as irregular retrieves do.

Full-Sink/Weighted Streamer

Of all the possible presentations, the one that requires the greatest will to use is the weighted fly with a high-density, full-sink line. Let's be honest here—it's just plain boring, tiring fishing. You thought trying to cast a soaking-wet Bunny Fly was a drag, but you'll beg to go back to it after this experience, especially during windy conditions. This presentation has its place, though, when conditions are tough, particularly during cold fronts. In these circumstances, it may very well be the only option, and that's the only time I resort to using it.

So, now that you know how I really feel, when do I have to resort to this combination? My spring trips to Canada are based around the highly coveted post-spawn period, and it's all about timing. Get there too early and the fish are still deep. Arrive too late and the pike will have begun to scatter back into deeper waters. Even when you time it right, you're faced with the possibility of cold fronts putting the fish down.

There are two options. First, don't go. Now, that won't work, so we have to use the second option—deal with the inclement weather and unfavorable conditions. You can hope you won't have too many bad days, but it can save a trip if you can deal with them.

My last trip to Canada was seven days long. It started with two beautiful days that gave way to cold, driving rains and temperatures in the forties. If you think going from the upper seventies down to the forties is a shock to your system, imagine what it does to pike. While the first two days provided perfect conditions, the following two days found the pike retreating to deeper, warmer water.

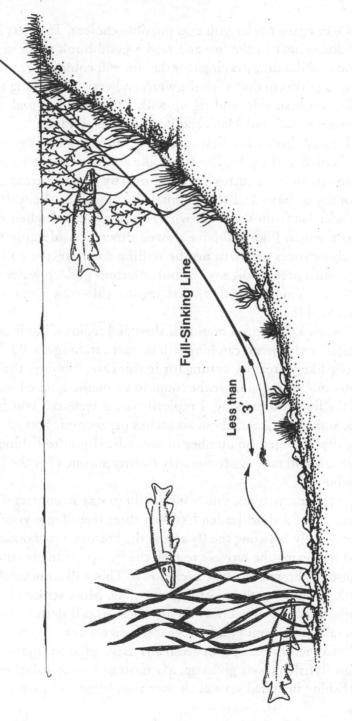

Weighted streamer presentation: Full-sinking line.

Once again I offer you two possible choices. The first is to stay in the lodge next to the fire and read a good book while sipping a hot toddy, all the time praying that the sun will come out the next day. Or you can dress to deal with the weather, because it's going to be a long, cold, wet boat ride, and rig up with a full-sink line and a handful of Clouser's Half-and-Halfs and Popovic's Jiggy Flies.

I never choose the first option, because I'm just as stubborn and pigheaded as the pike. Locating pike after strong fronts have pushed through only requires probing nearby deeper areas around the mouths of bays and the channels leading into them. Pike seldom wander far from the areas where they've staged when the weather was warmer. Pike will have slowed down considerably under these circumstances and will not be willing to chase your flies very far. You must present pike with your offerings in deep water with a slow manner. You guessed it, that means full-sink lines and heavily weighted flies.

The sink/sink presentation is slow and tedious, but it can mean the difference between catching fish or just catching a cold. You should probe likely areas by casting (or in this case, lobbing) the fly as far as you can. Once again, use the countdown method, based on the density of the line you're using. I typically use a type six, which means the line sinks at a rate of about six inches per second. You need to double the depth to get the number of seconds. If you're fishing ten feet of water, it will take approximately twenty seconds for the line to reach the bottom.

In these situations, you want the fly to stay in contact with the bottom, so use a short leader, less than three feet. Begin your retrieve by very slowly crawling the fly across the bottom. Occasionally lift your rod tip during the retrieve to pick the fly up off the bottom, and then pause to allow it to settle back down. This will sometimes provoke a strike from even the most negative pike. Most strikes, however, will come as you slowly crawl the fly back. You'll need to vary your retrieval speeds until you find what the pike want.

This method has produced many large pike for me on days when most flyfishers have given up. My most memorable day with this type of fishing included seven fish over twenty pounds, with one of those

There are many ways to fish streamers that are effective when used in the right situation.

pushing the thirty-pound mark and stretching the tape to almost fifty inches. Now, I ask you, would you like a hot toddy or do you want to go fishing? The choice is yours!

As you can see, there are many ways to fish streamers, all of which are effective when used in the right situations. These certainly aren't all the options. They're simply the ones that have produced best for me. As I move on to divers, you'll see there are just as many combinations to fish them, as well. Many of them produce results that once were thought only possible with conventional tackle.

Divers

In the simplest terms, divers are flies that incorporate a collar on the front half of the fly, shaped to force the fly below the surface. A closer look exposes a fly capable of much more. Larry Dahlberg describes his Dahlberg Diver series of flies as an "underwater delivery system" for Flashabou, but they also deliver many other materials. These include rabbit strips, feathers, Icelandic sheep hair, and Bozo Hair, all of which spring to life behind the diving head. Divers are extremely versatile flies that can cover a wide range of conditions. They're as much at home below the surface as they are on top.

.Not just a delivery system, divers attract predatory fish by moving and pushing water. This element plays well to the pike's lateral line, which detects prey by sound and pulse waves transmitted through the water and alerts the pike to the fly's presence before it's even seen. Divers excel at displacing water.

One day I was fishing water so dirty that if we were to catch a fish, we'd have to hit it on the head. Where I was fishing isn't important, but the conditions we faced are. There'd been lots of rain prior to my arrival, and the water was on the rise and dirty, very dirty. Standing knee-deep in water, I couldn't see past where my waders met the water.

With four of us in the group, we elected to try different patterns until somebody started catching fish. I started out with my usual Bunny Fly, but it didn't take long to figure out that somebody was catching fish while the rest of us were shrugging our shoulders. While all the other offerings failed to produce, the diver was moving fish on a regular basis. We'd all fished divers occasionally and done very well, and in less than an hour, the entire group had switched to them.

While the first hour produced a total of six pike—all taken by the lucky angler who'd started with a diver—the following three-hour foray in this small lake produced more than twenty-three pike in excess of forty-five inches and a monster fifty-two-inch pike that weighed close to thirty-five pounds.

During the heat of the fishing, several of us switched back to streamers just to see what would happen. No fish were taken on streamers that day. The pike just couldn't see them or detect their presence with their lateral line. This was the day that divers earned their standing with me. The diver's ability to displace water allowed the pike to locate, track down, and eat it in conditions that otherwise would have made for a very long day indeed.

Diver Types

Divers come in many sizes, shapes, and materials. There are now divers designed specifically for many freshwater and saltwater species. Some are short and bulky, while others are sleek and long. As with other types of flies, there are divers that imitate and those that attract. While the color schemes vary, along with the overall size and shape of the head and collar, they're all built to dive, displace, and deliver.

Clipped deer hair is the preferred choice of material for the diving head. Deer hair is lightweight, making it is easy to cast, while its hollow core makes it highly buoyant. It's dyed in many colors for use in designing flies that resemble naturals. Hot, bright, flashy colors are also available for attractor patterns. The only disadvantage to deer-hair divers is their vulnerability to the pike's razor-sharp teeth. Pike have been known to make rather quick work of these flies, particularly if they're tied poorly.

One alternative to deer hair is foam. You can purchase foam diver heads made by Edgewater Foam from fly shops and catalog companies. Foam is durable—kind of like a chew toy for pike. Foam also floats well. Sounds like the problem is solved, but it's not without a price and that comes in the form of weight. Foam heads weigh considerably more than their deer-hair counterparts. There are lighter-weight versions of foam diver heads on the market, but they lack durability. The choice is yours, but I personally prefer deer hair, due to its light weight.

Woolhead flies covered with silicone offer another alternative. Bob Popovic's silicone flies have diving lips much like you'd find on a Rapala lure. The diving lips are formed by spinning wool, in much the same manner as deer hair is spun, and giving the lip a rough shape. Then silicone is applied and allowed to dry, and the heads are shaped once more. The advantage of this design is the side-to-side action produced by the diving lip. It makes the fly more lifelike as it's stripped through the water.

One word of caution. If you're tying these flies yourself, the design of the head is critical. For the fly to track and fish properly, the diving collar and lip must be as close to perfect as you can make it. The result of a poorly trimmed diver will be a fly that doesn't ride upright, making the diving collar useless, or a diving lip that's not true to center, causing the fly to spin as it comes through the water. When fishing these patterns, it's a good idea to carry a pair of tying scissors with you, so you can do some fine-tuning on the water.

Diver Tactics

I like to break my diver fishing into the same four depth categories I described before—surface, subsurface, suspended (neutral-density), and bottom. To achieve these presentations, I again use different combinations of fly lines and leader lengths and match my retrieves to the presentation. First I'll discuss the four categories individually, and then I'll cover the specifics of how to make presentations throughout the water column.

Surface fishing with divers is very similar to fishing poppers. I use surface techniques in two areas. The first is over shallow water during the post-spawn and again in the fall when water temperatures permit shallow-water access.

The second location is over and around structure and cover. Structure comes in the form of break lines, rock reefs, and saddle areas near islands. The main cover I look for is cabbage and weed beds that push close to the surface but stop before they reach it. Other cover includes downed timber, old docks, rock piles, and boulders. When pike are actively feeding in these areas, they are close to the surface, usually in four feet of water or less. This makes them vulnerable to surface fishing with divers.

When I refer to fishing divers subsurface, I'm referring to "waking" the fly. I retrieve my diver just below the surface, with the fly pushing water as it moves. This presentation can be used in almost all areas and situations. I also use a diver and this presentation over open water when pike have forced baitfish toward the surface. This is an excellent way to imitate the behavior of a sick or crippled baitfish.

I learned the importance of waking divers by observation first and application second. On a local body of water where rainbows are regularly planted, the pike have become accustomed to being fed. Soon after the stocking trucks show up, the pike arrive in numbers. What happens next is best described as a free-for-all, as the pike bull through the stocker trout that are milling around as they try to become oriented to their new environment. Talk about a rude introduction.

Many of the trout survive an initial attack, but are injured, and they wander around haplessly, tight to the surface. This is where my observation paid off. As I watched this spectacle, I noticed that pike naturally hone in on injured fish. Why would pike expend precious energy when they can capture and eat something that can't escape easily? The answer is, they don't.

So, I watched pike pick off those trout, as opposed to chasing healthy ones. The other thing I observed is that when a trout becomes injured, the other trout separate themselves from what will be the next item on the pike's menu. Now I was ready to fish, or so I thought.

I tried fishing large poppers around the perimeter of the action to no avail. Their motion just wasn't right. Even though I varied my retrieves, the pike paid little attention to my offering. I had a couple of divers with me, so I figured I would give them a try. Success. Waking my fly and swimming it erratically right at the surface and just below it resulted in several nice pike that afternoon. The action produced by the diver was the key to getting the pike to respond.

Divers also allow me to use a neutral-density approach to flyfishing for suspended pike. This method is very productive in conventional angling circles where large jerk-baits are weighted so they suspend at the desired depth. This is deadly on large pike and muskies. By using a diver and a sink-type fly line, flyfishers can make the same type of presentation. Instead of adding weight to the fly, I choose a line with the right sink rate and change my leader length to adjust the depth.

Neutral-density presentations are best used over and around cover where pike are suspended. The inside and outside edges of weedlines are prime places for this presentation. Pike here will be suspended in and around the top or middle of cover, such as cabbage beds. Submerged trees, brush piles, and rock reefs with weed beds all hold suspended pike, particularly during warmer months and in the fall. This method really excels at bringing pike out of hiding. Keep in mind that the pike are suspended, not holding tight to the bottom. With this presentation, the fly hangs in front of them, hopefully suggesting that the pike should investigate an easy meal.

Last but not least is presenting a diver along the bottom to suggest prey that is swimming or crawling there. It's not a common approach for most flyfishermen, but it's one that can be quite effective when pike are feeding on things like crayfish, salamanders, and bottom-dwelling fish. Obviously, fishing a floating fly in this situation requires some

Submerged trees, brush piles, and rock reefs with weed beds all hold suspended pike.

special presentation tactics. In the next section, I'll discuss covering the water with divers from top to bottom. You'll be surprised at the presentations you can create with divers.

Floating Line/Diver

When you're wade fishing and casting back toward shallow water with a diver, use a floating line and the standard leader length of six to eight feet. Using a basic, straight retrieve, strip the fly back using short, sharp strips followed by a brief pause, fishing it very much like a popper.

If there's an abundance of aquatic or terrestrial vegetation, use the popper-style retrieve while the fly is in the vegetation. After the fly reaches open water, switch from the basic retrieve to diving mode—make three to four long, steady strips, forcing the fly downward. Follow each series of strips with a brief pause, allowing the fly to surface.

If this retrieve fails to produce, omit the pause and swim the fly just below the surface with a steady, straight retrieve. This imitates the waking action of a nervous fish being pursued through shallow water. Waking the fly requires you to shorten your leader down to four to six feet, depending on the diving collar of the fly. The shorter leader keeps your fly close to the surface while you use the swimming retrieve.

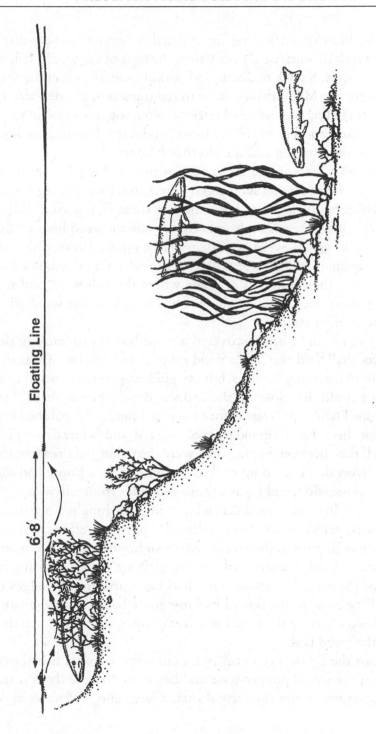

Floating Line

6-8'

Diver presentation: Floating line.

I also like to use a floating line with a diver over weed beds that don't quite reach the surface. Directly over the tops of the weeds, fish the fly popper-style. Switch to diving and waking the fly as it clears the edge of the weeds. Many strikes occur in the transition to open water. This tactic, including the change of retrieve, often triggers a violent response. This presentation is one of my most productive for summertime pike in the early morning and late afternoon hours.

My most memorable afternoon of pike fishing I owe to fishing divers over and around submerged vegetation. I was fishing Knee Lake in Manitoba during the early-summer transition period. Pike were leaving their post-spawn haunts to relocate on weed beds in eight to ten feet of water—weed beds that were a jungle. Presenting standard pike streamers meant I'd spend more time cleaning weeds from my fly and leader than fishing. But that's where the fish were, and if I was going to experience good fishing, I had to get out the weed whackers or use another strategy.

My guide and I had discovered a weed bed approximately the size of a football field that held a good number of large fish. I was stuck in the rut of throwing Bunnies, but my guide suggested I switch to something I could fish closer to the surface. Remembering that I'd picked up some Dahlberg Divers before the trip, I hurriedly searched my gear bag for them. I had a grand total of two red-and-white divers! I found myself torn between hoping they were the ticket and dreading the fact that divers don't stand up well to the pike's teeth. I only had the two in my possession, and I was a thousand miles from a fly shop.

After tying one on and throwing it into the jungle, I began a series of short, rapid strips that produced a popping effect without the diver hanging up in the weeds. After an hour or so I had taken several decent fish but none of the big girls we'd seen cruising in and out of the area. My guide and I had been probing the edges of the weedline close to the boat. I had my guide back the boat away from the weeds, leaving thirty to forty feet of open water between the boat and the weed bed.

I cast the fly twenty to thirty feet into the weeds. I fished over the tops of the weeds popper-style and began to dive the fly as it reached the open water. On my second cast, a large surge of water appeared behind the fly as it reached open water. Switching my retrieve from popper mode to dive mode had prompted a quick, decisive response from a pike that put a delightful bend in my nine-weight rod.

After covering the outer perimeter of the weed bed, I put my rod down to reflect on what I'd just experienced.

My guide looked up at me calmly, smiled, and said, "That's seventeen pike over forty inches!"

"That's more than I've caught all week!" I replied.

My guide snickered back, "Yeah, too bad you have to go home tomorrow!"

There's nothing worse than a guide with sick sense of humor.

While my two divers took a severe beating, they stood up to the punishment well enough to allow me to finish that afternoon of fishing. Rest assured, I carry plenty of divers with me today!

Fishing a diver with a floating line allows you to cover most shallow-water situations and even some open-water areas where popper-style and waking tactics work. It doesn't allow you to reach suspended pike or pike holding tight to the bottom, even in fairly shallow water. For these presentations, you must use sink-tip and full-sink lines. Using those types of lines, many presentations have been developed that were once thought to be beyond the realm of flyfishing.

Sink-Tip Line/Diver

Using sink-tip lines with divers is one of my favorite and most effective ways to catch pike and muskies on the fly. I've won several local muskie tournaments using this presentation, while competing against anglers using conventional gear!

This neutral-density presentation is achieved by fishing a floating fly (in this case, a diver) with a sink-tip line. Similar methods have been extremely productive for conventional anglers and this technique is quickly catching on with flyfishers.

A sink-tip line allows me to make a vertical presentation and fish the water column at different depths. I typically use a specific sink-tip length and leader length to match the depth of the water I'm fishing. In water less than eight feet deep, a five-foot tip is ample, while depths of over ten feet require a fifteen-foot tip. I use a sink rate of three to four

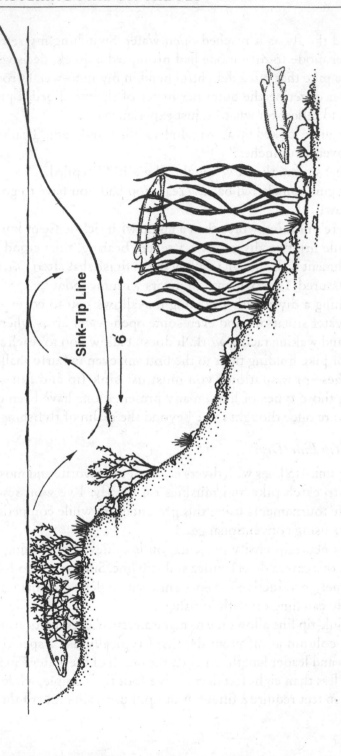

Diver presentation: Sink-tip line.

inches per second for shallow water and five to six for deeper water, counting the line down to the desired depth before I begin my retrieve.

Leader lengths are critical here as well. The longer the leader, the greater the amount of water you can cover in the column. Keep in mind that long leaders prevent good contact between you and your fly, making strikes harder to detect. The closer the fly is to the sink-tip, the less float time you'll get, but greater contact is maintained and strikes are easier to detect. On my sink-tip setups, I use a six-foot leader, which allows a four-foot float for the fly.

Let's assume for a moment that you're fishing in eight feet of water to suspended pike holding around the five-foot mark. You're fishing a diver with a six-foot leader and a sink-tip line that has a sink rate of six inches per second. Where does that leave you?

First, you want to allow your line to sink down below the pike. At six inches per second, your line will sink a foot every two seconds. Twelve seconds will be necessary for your line to travel six feet. Always allow an extra two-count to compensate for the floating fly and leader, which slow the sink rate slightly. At this point, begin your retrieve.

Give your line three long, fluid strips to drive the diver down toward the depth of the fish. Then pause and let the fly float ever so slowly back toward the surface. This takes some practice and a great deal of patience. Once the fly reaches the surface, allow it to rest motionless for a second before repeating the sequence. Many strikes occur as the fly floats up or immediately after you begin to dive the fly again.

If you're not getting strikes, tweak your presentation by altering the length of your leader. Start by shortening it, because getting no response typically signals that the pike is unwilling to give chase or leave its cover. A three-foot leader holds your diver closer to the tip of the line and keeps it suspended in the water column. This is a true neutral-density presentation—the fly just kind of hangs there, tethered to the sink-tip line.

Use the same retrieve for this subsurface tactic as you would when fishing the diver on the surface. Since you can't see the fly reach the end of its float toward the surface, you must count the up-float. With most deer-hair divers, the up-float is around six inches per second, depending on the quality of the fly. You can speed the process by applying a liberal amount of floatant or drying crystals to your fly. It's always a good idea to test your fly first in water that's shallow enough for you to establish the count rate.

In most cases, you'll get the best response when the fly is fished on a leader that's long enough for the fly to return to the surface. Over the years, this presentation and variations of it have accounted for over ninety percent of the tiger muskies I've caught. This neutral-density strategy has proven itself as a big-fish producer spring, summer, and fall. I've taken tigers to forty-seven inches, pike to fifty-two inches, and muskies to fifty inches this way. And I've moved even bigger fish that missed the fly as they savagely attacked it near the surface.

The first time you see a monster pike settle in beneath your fly as it slowly floats toward the surface, I think you'll agree on how effective and exciting this method of flyfishing can be.

Full-Sink Line/Diver

I think I've already made my feelings clear about using full-sink fly lines. I just don't like fishing them! But once again, there are occasions where their use becomes necessary. An alternative is to use longer sink-tips, twenty-four to thirty feet in length. One of the big knocks on sink-tips is the hinging effect, where a belly forms in the line causing different sink rates for the tip and midsection of the fly line. Full-sinking lines keep the fly at a constant depth, if the fly is being retrieved directly.

The one time I'll use a full-sink fly line with a diver is when I find neutral to negative pike in fairly shallow water. Fished in the shallows on short, two- to three-foot leaders, divers can be kept tight to the bottom where pike don't have to move far or expend much energy to catch and eat the fly. This combination allows for a slow, deliberate presentation, during which the fly can be dug into the bottom as it is retrieved, raising a mud cloud that looks very similar to a fleeing crayfish or other bottom dweller.

A few years ago, while fishing on Wollaston Lake in Saskatchewan, I came across several large pike holding in three feet of water on a shallow flat between a couple of small islands. These pike were large enough that, even after exhausting my normal routine and presentations, I couldn't pass them by. It was time for some experimenting.

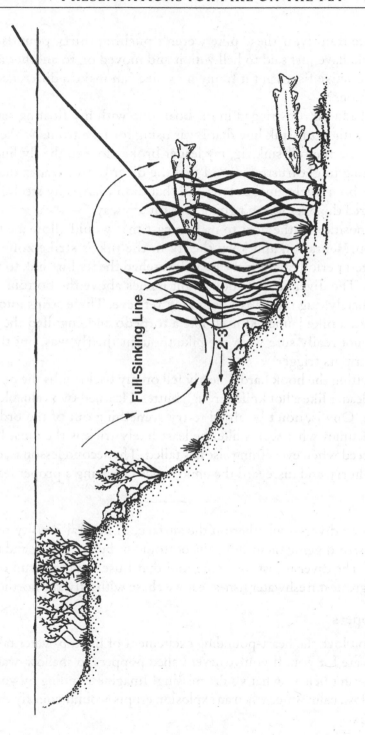

Diver presentation: Full-sinking line.

Quite frankly, if these pike weren't pushing thirty pounds each, I would have just said to hell with it and moved on to another area and more active fish. Isn't it funny how size can make a difference in our decisions?

I had two rods rigged in the boat, one with my floating setup and one with a full-sink line that I was using for lake trout. While tying a diver on the full-sink rig, my leader broke close to the fly line. I was starting to get frustrated, so I tied the diver onto a leader that might have been twelve inches long and that didn't have any steel. I guess I figured the pike weren't going to eat it anyway.

I positioned the boat to make a cast that would allow me to angle my presentation and keep the fly in the pike's strike zone for the longest period possible. I cast and watched the fly line sink to the bottom. The diver settled about eight inches above the bottom and immediately dug into it as I began my retrieve. Three strips into the retrieve, a pike launched itself like a torpedo and engulfed the fly. I'm still not really sure what the pike thought the fly was, but the tactic did trip its trigger.

Setting the hook hard, I nearly fell on my backside as the pike sliced my leader like a hot knife through butter. I learned two valuable lessons here. One is, don't be afraid to try something out of the ordinary—sometimes what seems like the least likely trick is the most likely to succeed when everything else has failed. The second lesson is, don't be in a hurry and disregard the importance of having a proper leader!

―――――――――――

Fishing divers—whether on the surface, in neutral-density presentations, or digging them along the bottom—is both exciting and productive. The diver is just one more tool that I use in my pursuit of one of the greatest freshwater fishes that we chase with a fly, the northern pike.

Poppers

If you love the heart-pounding excitement of the top-water take, poppers are for you. If you've never fished poppers to shallow-water pike, you can't believe what you're missing! Imagine standing by yourself in shallow, calm water when an explosion erupts around your fly that looks very much like someone threw in a kitchen sink. Now you have a good idea what it's like when a pike blows up on your popper. I had one client describe it as the most nerve-racking experience he ever enjoyed.

Today's poppers are constructed from a variety of materials but are most commonly made from clipped deer hair or foam. As you know, there are tradeoffs with each. Deer-hair poppers are extremely light-weight, but foam is considerably tougher. For what it's worth, I fish both. My favorite patterns include Popovic's Bangers and Stewart's Dancing Frog.

Poppers come in a multitude of shapes and sizes. Some have flat faces designed to make a loud popping sound as they're retrieved. Others have a cupped face, which disturbs large amounts of water.

Like other patterns, poppers come in shapes, colors, and profiles that imitate natural food, such as baitfish and frogs, or they may imitate nothing and work as an attractor pattern that brings pike in with color and noise. The bottom line here is that pike are most often attracted to poppers not by how they look but by how they sound. Noise is an important part of fishing poppers—it calls out for attention by saying, "Here I am, come eat me."

Popper Tactics

For obvious reasons, poppers are most effective when pike are feeding near the surface, either in the shallows or over the top of deep-water cover, such as weeds that grow near the surface. During the post-spawn, pike spend a great deal of time in the warming shallows where popper fishing excels. Pike are super aggressive, leading to some phenomenal top-water action. When the summer heat drives pike to deeper water and weed beds push toward the surface, early morning and late evening can find pike feeding near the surface over those areas.

Other habitats appropriate for fishing poppers include areas of deadfall, reeds, cattails, and any other location with quick access to the surface where pike can ambush prey. Aquatic vegetation or terrestrial vegetation that becomes flooded during high-water periods is also conducive to poppers.

One of my more memorable top-water days was on a large Canadian lake during the post-spawn period. Unusually high spring waters more

Aquatic vegetation or terrestrial vegetation that becomes flooded is also conducive to poppers.

than doubled the size of the bays we'd fished in previous years. These high waters flooded out onto the tundra, and many bushes and shrubs were covered by water. The pike didn't seem to mind too much, since they readily took advantage of the new cover. The pike were so thick, the bushes quivered from the fish moving through them. The problem was that the bushes were just as thick and made any presentation—other than poppers—difficult.

We were on one of the top bays in the lake, and it had all the key ingredients we look for. Several small creeks that fed the back of the bay had swollen and breached their banks. A soft, dark, mucky bottom, flooded grasses, and brush piles meant there were plenty of ambush points. We just needed a fly that we could present in this tundra jungle without hanging up on every piece of crud protruding from the water. The obvious choice was a popper with a stout weed guard!

Probing the open pockets with a popper was eye opening, to say the least. When I cast to the openings and gave the popper a couple of twitches, nearby brush would begin to shiver and shake as pike rushed my offering. Fighting large pike in tight quarters requires a strong heart and the agility to act quickly in what becomes a humorous ballet

Fighting large pike in tight quarters requires a strong heart and the agility to act quickly.

between man and pike. I heard more than one chuckle from other anglers fishing the area in boats, but they were using conventional tackle and throwing hardware that prevented them from fishing where the fish were.

Floating Line/Popper

There are two ways I like to fish poppers—the traditional presentation with a floating line and a non-traditional presentation that uses a short sink-tip line. I refer to this latter presentation as the big bang! The traditional popper presentation works well in clear, calm water, while the big bang excels in less favorable conditions with slightly choppy water or water that is dirty, providing little visibility.

With the traditional presentation, I use a leader between six and eight feet in length. My presentations always start with a long pause before I actually begin stripping the fly back. The length of the pause is measured by simply allowing the water to calm after the fly hits the surface. The retrieve is variable until I find the response I'm looking for. I start with one firm strip to produce the pop and follow each strip with a pause. If this fails to produce, I try a series of short, hard strips (usually two or three), again followed by a pause.

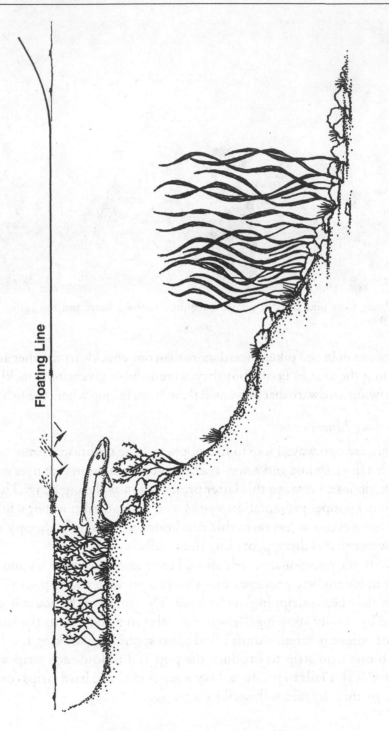

Floating Line

Popper presentation: Floating line.

Most strikes occur right after the pause, as you begin the retrieve again. Pike typically settle in just behind and underneath the fly before they take it. For super-aggressive pike, I find that a constant retrieve with no pause works best. Aggressive pike will usually take the fly whether you pause or not. I actually believe these pike enjoy the pursuit of the fly.

Sink-tip Line/Popper

Sometimes when pike are holding in slightly deeper water or over submerged cover, they're still willing to feed near the surface. This is when I utilize the big-bang retrieve. The big-bang retrieve uses a short, five-foot, sink-tip line and a five-foot leader. The short sink-tip helps me drive the popper harder and deeper into the water, creating much more disturbance, both visually and through sound vibrations.

The idea is to create as much disturbance as possible to alert any nearby pike to the presence of the fly. This presentation excels in dirty water where visual provocation is minimal and I have to rely heavily on sound to stimulate the pike. Use of this retrieve is an excellent way to search water, as well, since it favors the use of the two items pike rely on most heavily to feed, their keen eyesight and their well-developed lateral line system.

Like most off-the-wall ideas, I stumbled across this method. I was fishing a lake far from home in less-than-ideal circumstances. The water was high and dirty, and fishing was tough. The pike were there and very aggressive, but the water was so dirty I basically had to hit them on the head before they could see the fly. Even though there were plenty of pike around, they were scattered. I caught some fish, but I knew there had to be a better way.

I was using a short sink-tip line and weighted fly. This setup made sense to me, since I had to place the fly right on top of the fish. As it often does when fishing is slow, my mind began to wander. I tried to think of a way I could create some noise with my presentation to stimulate the pike's lateral line to help them locate my offerings better. Digging through my bag, I found a handful of Popovic's poppers and figured they might be worth a shot. The problem was that I had been in such a hurry to get on the water that day, I'd left behind the spare spool with my floating line.

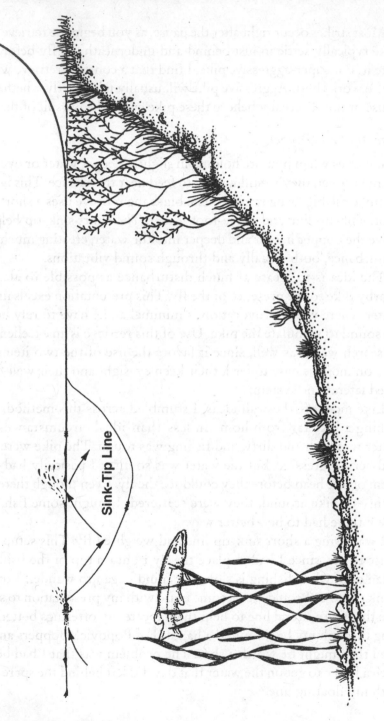

Popper presentation: Sink-tip line.

Well, it was only a five-foot tip and I figured it was still worth a try. What I found was that the sink-tip actually helped create more noise and surface disturbance than fishing the popper with a floating line! The only downfall was that it required a longer pause before the popper resurfaced. I shortened my leader down to five or six feet, so the popper would return to the surface a little more quickly, and found that shortening the leader created an even better popping action and more noise!

After a couple of adjustments, my new setup was ready for the test. I cast where I'd caught several fish earlier using streamers. Three strips into my retrieve, the water erupted in what looked like the scene from *The Hunt for Red October* when the submarine surfaces in a hurry. Water went everywhere, and I was fast into a large pike. My heart was racing like I'd just run a marathon.

This presentation produced not just one strike but many others like it throughout the day. Altogether, I took twenty-three pike that ran from the rather ordinary thirty-inch variety to the super-sized, high-forty-inch version. They all fell for the sink-tip/popper combination. The following day I fished the same areas with a regular floating line with some success but nothing compared to what I'd experienced the day before. Disappointed, I switched back to the sink-tip line setup, and the action picked up sharply once again.

It seemed the more water that was disturbed and the noisier the presentation, the better the results. I have tried this presentation under more favorable conditions with mixed results. As I said earlier, this a good search presentation, but it really excels in dirty-water situations. Next time you find yourself in conditions where water clarity is a problem, give the big-bang presentation a try and see for yourself how important the pike's lateral line is when it comes to locating food under adverse conditions. Go ahead and make some noise!

Finish Your Retrieves!

I can't complete a discussion of presentations without talking about finishing your retrieve. Another big mistake I see anglers make in flyfishing for pike is picking up the line before they should! Both pike and muskies are notorious for following flies right up to the rod tip. On my last pike trip, my biggest pike, 50-plus inches of it, ate the fly literally within an arm's reach. Had I not finished stripping the fly all the way in, odds are pretty good I would never have caught that pike. It would have disappeared into the depths without my ever knowing that the fish was there, let alone interested in my fly! Never pick up your retrieve before the fly is close enough to see if there's a pike following it.

This is the number-one tip I can share with each and every one of you—extend and finish your retrieves. I personally guarantee you'll catch more fish! Strip your fly back until the fly-line-to-leader connection reaches your rod tip. At this point, simply roll your rod to the left or the right, twitch your rod, and pull the fly past your side to make certain there are no latecomers waiting to attack the fly at the last possible moment. I have converted more follows to strikes and subsequent hook-ups by using this one simple technique than all the others combined.

When you detect a follow and extend your retrieve in this manner, but the pike still doesn't strike, don't give up! If a pike has followed this far, chances are you can bank on the old adage of "curiosity killed the cat." Your first response should be to roll the rod side-to-side, from right to left and back again. All the time you're doing this, give the fly tantalizing twitches, trying to get the pike to pounce on it. If you're wade fishing and there's enough water between yourself and the shoreline, turn in a slow circle. This strange pike dance draws many curious stares from other anglers ... until the water erupts and a big pike is on.

Occasionally I get lazy and cut my retrieves short, but it doesn't take long before a big pike reminds me to finish my retrieves by charging a fly that's no longer there. When you're getting lots of follows, slow down, bring the end of your line to the rod tip, and extend your retrieve. It can be hard enough to get a really big pike up to eat the first time, and your success rate declines rapidly with each try that follows. Anybody want to dance?

Sight Fishing and Spotting Pike

Many pike waters are clear, pristine bodies of water that offer prime conditions to sight fish. There is nothing more exhilarating to me than stalking big pike in clear water. The stalk, the presentation, and ultimately, the take are rewarding, to say the least! Very few fish will make your knees go weak and your heart skip a beat the way a big pike does when it explodes from a dead stop to engulf your fly at hyper speed ... while you watch.

The ability to spot fish in general, not just pike, is an art that will ultimately increase your success, no matter what species you pursue. For instance, being able to spot a school of cruising fish on the saltwater flats, identify them as bonefish, determine which direction they're moving, and make your presentation before they detect your presence greatly increases your chances of catching one. While pike don't travel in schools and prefer to hunt from cover, the ability to spot them before they spot you will also increase your odds of catching them.

Unless blind casting is the only option, I prefer to stalk pike and sight fish to them whenever possible. Not only is it more productive than blind casting, it is a hell of a lot more fun!

The first step in learning to spot fish is knowing their color scheme and the environment in which they live. Like so many predators, the pike's coloration allows them to blend in with their environment, making them difficult for predator and prey alike to detect. Around spawning time, the pike's fins turn blood red, and this makes them somewhat easier to spot when they're holding in a patch of green weeds.

Look for subtle color changes in the vegetation or bottom make-up when you're spotting pike. If you sense any difference, cast before proceeding any farther. Anything that looks unusual in shape or size is always worth a cast or two. Sometimes that clump of weeds is just that, but there are many times when that clump of weeds has fins and swims.

Shadows probably give away a pike's location more than any other factor. On bright, sunny days, all objects give off a shadow, pike included. Just as I do when I'm fishing around vegetation, I watch for irregularities in shapes on the bottom. Seemingly inanimate objects, like the shadow of a log or rock, often end up being a pike. I always look at the size, shape, and silhouette of shadows and check for irregularities. I treat any shadow as if it were a pike, until I'm certain otherwise!

Movement is an obvious key to spotting pike when you have bright skies and flat water. Most days, a lake isn't flat for long, making spotting

Shadows probably give away a pike's location more than any other factor.

pike suspended below the surface difficult at best. Once again, I'm always looking for shadows that move or just seem out of place.

Spotting pike is an art that is learned over time by trial and error. Some anglers pick it up faster than others, but most learn over time. Whether you learn to spot pike by movement, shadows, color variations, or all three, the end result offers you the opportunity to catch more fish. But there are a few last keys to spotting pike we need to discuss.

Obviously, the higher your vantage point above the water, the easier it is to spot pike. If you're in a boat, you have a definite advantage over wading fishermen, due to the angle. With wade fishing, your ability to sight fish decreases significantly as the water depth increases.

Sunglasses! Not cheap, throwaway sunglasses, but a quality pair of polarized glasses. These are your most important tool for spotting pike. Polarized glasses cut the glare off the water's surface, allowing you to see into it. Even on the darkest days when clouds hang low overhead, polarized glasses help you see into the pike's underwater world. Spending a little extra money on a quality pair of sunglasses will save you lots of time and frustration when you're trying to spot fish.

One last point. By learning to spot pike when conditions permit, you can anticipate where pike will be when you can't see them. Some of the rivers I fish are quite turbid, making sight fishing almost impossible. In these rivers, I rely heavily on what I've learned when I could see pike in other rivers. So, your ability to spot fish is important not only in clear water, but it also pays off when conditions are less favorable.

Learning to sight any fish is an acquired art that won't happen overnight and can only improve, like any other part of fishing, by spending more time on the water!

Overview

This chapter is the heart of the book. I've shared personal tricks I've learned while spending many frustrating hours, days, and years observing and experimenting. And I've passed on information that I've learned from other hardcore pike addicts. Each one of these presentations, retrieves, and tactics has its proper time and place, and each is deadly effective when done properly.

In the following chapter I'll discuss the fly patterns I've found most effective for pike. As you read about these patterns, keep in mind the options you have to present each and under what circumstances they're likely to succeed. Every time I see a new, innovative pattern, my first thought is, *I bet pike will eat that*. My mind immediately begins to move to the many presentation possibilities the pattern has to offer. When you begin to think this way, you will know that you, too, have become a pike-on-the-fly addict.

SIX

FLIES FOR PIKE

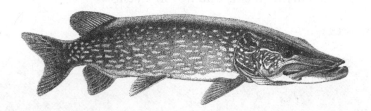

T he selection of patterns in this chapter includes the flies I use most commonly. Streamers make up the bulk of the patterns, because they imitate what pike most often eat. Although many of the patterns are given in colors that imitate naturals in the areas I fish, you can adjust those colors for your local waters. You can also change the colors to create attractor patterns. I've given suggestions for effective optional colors in the notes at the end of the recipes. Be creative and have some fun. After all, that's what makes this part of our sport so enjoyable.

All these flies can be tied on hooks in sizes to match the equipment you'll be using. The standard hook size for most of my pike flies is #3/0, but if you use lighter tackle, you may wish to tie them in smaller sizes. As a general guideline, I make the following recommendations for fly sizes and the rods that can best handle them. Hook sizes #2-#6 can be handled well with a seven-weight rod. Hook sizes #2-#2/0 are better with an eight-weight rod. Hooks in the size range of #1/0-#4/0 are best handled with a nine-weight. When throwing flies of monstrous proportions in hook sizes of #4/0-#6/0, a ten-weight rod will work best.

The materials used will also greatly affect the weight and casting characteristics of your flies. Most synthetic material is lighter in weight, so you can cast larger flies with lighter rods. This is also the case with deer-hair patterns, since these flies are lightweight. Many of the natural materials, such as rabbit fur, soak up copious amounts of water that add weight, making larger rods a must.

Since this book is not intended to be a fly-tying manual, I have not included tying instructions, but I do have a couple of tips. Due to the large size of many of these flies and their weight, I prefer to use salt-water hooks. You can substitute comparable bronze hooks, if you wish. For epoxied heads, I recommend a five-minute epoxy, such as Z-Poxy, which dries quickly and doesn't yellow.

Streamers

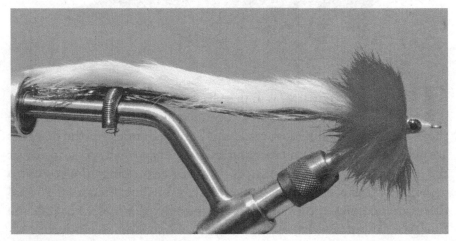

Bunny Fly

Bunny Fly

The Bunny Fly is my version of the American Express Card—I never leave home without it! This fly has so many positive attributes that it's been my number-one producer for years. With its shape, size, action, and abundant color options, the Bunny Fly can cover any pike-fishing situation, from top to bottom. Yes, I've gone so far as to treat the rabbit fur with drying crystals to fish a Bunny Fly on the surface, with devastating results.

The rabbit strip comes to life in the water and has a very suggestive action that beckons pike to investigate. The overall size and the colors can be changed to suggest anything and everything, from leeches to baitfish to crayfish. While I don't elect to do so, many anglers add weight in the form of dumbbell eyes or cones. For me, the extra weight is too much. When wet, these patterns already outweigh most of the trout I catch!

The durability of this fly is phenomenal. Pike can chew on this fly like a dog chewing on its favorite rawhide, without destroying it. To add even more durability, I always use epoxy on the heads to protect the thread from the pike's sharp teeth. Whether you fish this fly large or small, black or white, the important thing is to make sure you have plenty of them with you.

Recipe: Bunny Fly

Hook: Straight eye, extra strong, standard length, forged, stainless, e.g. Tiemco TMC 811S
Size: 2-3/0
Thread: White single-strand nylon floss
Tail: White rabbit strip, 4☐ to 5☐ long, red Krystal Flash
Body: Red rabbit strip, 4☐ to 5☐ long, palmered
Eyes: Red prismatic stick-on, 3.5 mm
Head: White single-strand nylon floss, built up, epoxied
Weed Guard (optional): Mason hard mono, 25 lb.

Notes: This pattern is sold by Umpqua as Barry's Pike Fly. Color scheme suggestions include solid colors such as black, white, yellow, chartreuse, and pink. Two-tone combinations also excel, and my favorites include a red body with a white tail (given here) and a red body with a yellow tail.

Bunnyceiver

This hybrid is a cross between the standard Bunny Fly and a Lefty's Deceiver. It was designed to decrease the weight of the Bunny by using the lighter-weight bucktail from the front of a Lefty's Deceiver with the rabbit-fur tail of a Bunny Fly. The result is a fly that is lighter and easier to cast, but still maintains much of the action of the Bunny Fly.

I've been using this hybrid for the last couple of years with good success. The slimmer profile of this pattern is more suggestive of cylindrical-shaped baitfish and works well in areas where pike feed on whitefish and suckers, for example. The only downfall of this pattern is that it lacks the durability of the Bunny Fly. Pike tend to chew up the bucktail more quickly than the rabbit strip.

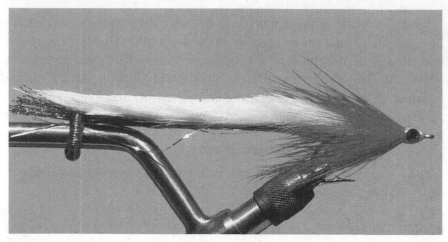

Bunnyceiver

Recipe: Bunnyceiver

Hook: Straight eye, extra strong, standard length, forged, stainless, e.g. Tiemco TMC 811S

Size: 2/0-4/0

Thread: White single-strand nylon floss

Tail: White rabbit strip, 4□ to 5□ long, red Krystal Flash, silver Flashabou

Body: Silver Mylar braid

Collar: Red bucktail

Eyes: Red prismatic stick-on, 3.5 mm

Head: White single-strand nylon floss, built up, epoxied

Weed Guard (optional): Mason hard mono, 25 lb.

Notes: Color scheme suggestions include white, black, and chartreuse for solid-color patterns. Red/white (given here), red/yellow, and gray/white excel for two-tone flies, with red and gray being the collar colors.

Barr's Bouface

This is another excellent lightweight option when casting a Bunny Fly is too much for your gear or your mood. The Bouface has a marabou collar and is tied on a bronze hook, making the fly significantly lighter.

As usual, there's a trade-off. The Bouface's durability is not as good as flies tied with a rabbit-strip collar.

I typically use a Bouface when I'm fishing water that both pike and bass inhabit. The Bouface is an excellent bass pattern that doubles for pike. Since I do most of my bass fishing with a seven-weight rod, the Bouface is a better choice than a Bunny Fly.

Barr's Bouface

Recipe: Barr's Bouface

Hook: Bass bug hook, straight eye, fine wire, wide gape, forged, bronze, e.g. Tiemco TMC 8089
Size: 2-6
Thread: White 3/0 nylon
Tail: White rabbit strip, 2□ to 4□ long, topped with red Flashabou or Krystal Flash
Collar: Red marabou
Head: White 3/0 nylon thread, built-up, epoxied
Weed Guard (optional): Mason hard mono, 25 lb.

Notes: Color schemes vary from match-the-hatch naturals of black, white, gray, and chartreuse to attractor color combinations of red/white (given here), red/yellow, and yellow/black, with the first color listed being the collar.

Lefty's Deceiver

Lefty's Deceiver

This pattern might very well be the single most successful streamer ever created. It's that good! Deceivers can imitate so many different baitfish that they have become a staple in almost every angler's fly box. It has been said that Deceivers have been responsible for catching more species of fish than any other pattern.

Covering the water from top to bottom ensures success throughout the season, and Deceivers are one of the best patterns for this. They're also lightweight and easy to cast. To date, my best success is with all-white patterns tied in larger sizes of #3/0 to #5/0. You can vary the overall shape of the fly by adding or subtracting materials.

Recipe: Lefty's Deceiver

Hook: Straight eye, extra strong, standard length, forged, stainless, e.g. Tiemco TMC 811S
Size: 1/0-5/0
Thread: White single-strand nylon floss
Tail: 6-8 white saddle feathers, pearl Krystal Flash
Body: Chartreuse single-strand nylon floss or silver tinsel
Collar: Chartreuse bucktail top, white bucktail bottom
Throat: Red Krystal Flash

Eyes: Chartreuse prismatic stick-on, 2.5 mm
Head: Chartreuse single-strand nylon floss, built up, epoxied

Notes: Here again, color schemes run the gamut from match-the-hatch naturals of black, gray, and white to attractor colors of red/white, red/yellow, and chartreuse/white (given here). The lighter color always represents the bottom color in these combinations.

Roger's Big-Eye Baitfish

Roger's Big-Eye Baitfish

Although similar to a Deceiver, this pattern offers a larger profile and a different shape, suggesting a stouter meal. I've had a great deal of success with this pattern in lakes where bluegills are on the pike's menu. This pattern incorporates the use of highly reflective prismatic tape for the cheek area over which the eye is placed, making it highly visible in low-light or dirty-water situations.

Marabou can be used in place of the typical bucktail collar to change the overall profile to suggest different types of baitfish. Synthetics, such as Ultra Hair, can also be used in place of the bucktail, resulting in a fly that weighs less and sheds water more easily. Of course, synthetics lack the action of natural materials.

Recipe: Roger's Big-Eye Baitfish

Hook: Round, straight eye, 3X heavy, 3X wide, 2X short, forged, black nickel, e.g. Tiemco TMC 600SP Super Point

Size: 1/0-3/0

Thread: White single-strand nylon floss

Tail: 4-6 white saddle feathers

Collar: Gray bucktail top over pearl Flashabou (can be topped with peacock herl), white bucktail bottom

Cheeks: Silver Witchcraft prismatic tape

Eyes: Orange prismatic stick-on, 3.5 mm

Throat: Red wool

Head: White single-strand nylon floss, colored with black Pantone pen, epoxied

Notes: My favorite color scheme with this pattern is called Hot Tamale; it uses fluorescent red saddle feathers over fluorescent orange feathers, with a yellow collar and copper Flashabou, topped with peacock herl. Other color patterns to consider are blue/white, gray/white (given here), and green/yellow, with the lighter color on the bottom of the collar.

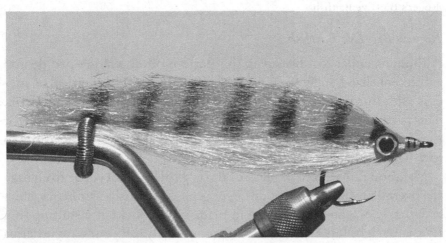

Emmons' Yak Fly

Emmons' Yak Fly

The Yak Fly offers a long, slender profile that is suggestive of many of the baitfish pike love to eat. It offers size in its length, but this successful pattern is lightweight and easy on the casting arm, even soaking wet. The yak hair takes Pantone pen markings well, and your imagination is the only limit on color schemes.

Recipe: Emmons' Yak Fly

Hook: Round, straight eye, 3X heavy, 3X wide, 2X short, forged, black nickel, e.g. Tiemco TMC 600SP Super Point
Size: 1/0-3/0
Thread: White single-strand nylon floss
Tail: White yak hair, pearl Flashabou
Body: Pearl braid
Top wing: Medium-blue yak hair
Bottom Wing: White yak hair
Gills: Red Synthetic Living Fiber
Head: White single-strand nylon floss, built up, colored with Pantone pen, epoxied
Eyes: Gold molded plastic, 3.5 mm

Notes: I tie this pattern in white and then use Pantone marking pens to shade or color the fly to match the local forage base. I also tie a chartreuse-and-white combination that I like to use as a basic probing fly. As with most streamers, the darker color—chartreuse in this case—is used on the top wing and the lighter color on the bottom wing.

Kintz's Bunker Fly

This is another large-profile pattern. Tied in appropriate colors, it can suggest anything from bluegill to shad. Originally designed for saltwater stripers, Bunker Flies can be weighted to cover deep-water situations. I regularly tie them both weighted and unweighted.

I started using this pattern for tiger muskies on a local lake that has shad from six- to twelve-inches long. While I'm not about to start throwing twelve-inch flies, I can imitate the smaller shad quite effectively with this pattern. I now use the Bunker Fly regularly on other waters, as well. By simply changing the colors, it can imitate different forage fish.

Kintz's Bunker Fly

Recipe: Kintz's Bunker Fly

Hook: Straight eye, extra strong, standard length, forged, stainless, e.g. Tiemco TMC 811S

Size: 3/0-5/0

Thread: White 6/0

Tail: 4-6 white saddle feathers, blue-gray bucktail, brown Streamer Hair, pearl Flashabou

Body: Pearl braided Mylar

Under Collar: Blue-gray bucktail, pearl Flashabou

Top Collar: Blue-gray bucktail

Top wing: Dark brown Streamer Hair

Eyes: White plastic doll eyes, 12 mm

Head: White 6/0 thread, built up, epoxied

Notes: I've been most successful with this pattern in natural colors. Gray-and-white (given here) excels as a generic baitfish imitation and covers most situations well. When more imitative colors fail, I've also done well with a version tied with a red topping and a white belly and tail.

D's Minnow

D's Minnow

This pattern was designed by my good friend Darrell Sickmon, of Aurora, Colorado. While the pattern has been altered from its original form, the idea behind the fly remains the same. Without a doubt, it's the fly's overall shape and size that makes it one of the most realistic patterns I've fished.

I break out the D's Minnow when pike get finicky on me and in areas where they've been fished over heavily. Late fall has also been a productive time to use this fly, and it has saved my neck more than once. While fishing Wollaston Lake in Saskatchewan, Canada, one early September, I had follow after follow with no hits. After exhausting my fly selection, I remembered I had some D's Minnows, but they were back at the lodge.

Returning to the bay the following day, I started out with a Bunny Fly and got those aggravating follows again. I switched over to a D's Minnow and fished it where a large pike had chased flies to the boat on numerous occasions the previous day. Sure enough, the pike followed the fly again. Only this time, she slowly opened her jaws and gently inhaled the fly. She was forty-nine inches in length. I now make sure I always have several D's Minnows with me on the water—not in my other bag.

Recipe: D's Minnow

Hook: Straight eye, extra strong, standard length, forged, stainless,
         e.g. Tiemco TMC 811S
Size: 1/0-3/0
Thread: White flat waxed nylon
Tail: Reflash tubing with blue-dun marabou through it
Body: Pearl Cactus Chenille
Under Wing: White Synthetic Living Fiber
Top Wing: Gray Synthetic Living Fiber, pearl Krystal Flash, topped
         with 6-8 strands of peacock herl
Gills: Red Synthetic Living Fiber
Head: White flat waxed nylon, built up, epoxied, pearl glitter on top
Eyes: Gold prismatic stick-on, 3.5 mm

Notes: Synthetic Living Fiber comes in many colors, allowing you to match the available food base. I've had great success with gray/white (given here) for most baitfish patterns, green/yellow for perch, and olive/orange/white for bluegill, with the lighter colors for the belly. This material readily takes Pantone markers, when barring or other markings are required for a realistic imitation.

Barry's Frizzy Baitfish

Barry's Frizzy Baitfish

I'm forever on the quest to build a better mousetrap. This generic but flashy baitfish pattern is quickly making its way up my favorites list. Combining both natural and synthetic materials, it's a lightweight yet durable baitfish pattern that has accounted for many big, finicky pike. In clear water, I prefer to use realistic colors. In dirty water, bright, flashy colors produce well. For pike feeding near the surface or in shallow water, I like to fish this pattern on a floating line. Suspended pike prefer it fished with a sink-tip line.

Recipe: Barry's Frizzy Baitfish

Hook: Straight eye, extra strong, standard length, forged, stainless, e.g. Tiemco TMC 811S
Size: 1/0-3/0
Thread: White single-strand nylon floss
Tail: White bucktail, silver Flashabou, pearl Flashabou
Body: Silver braid
Belly: White bucktail
Wing: Silver and pearl Flashabou, white bucktail, chartreuse Frizzy Fiber, peacock herl
Throat: Red Frizzy Fiber
Head: White single-strand nylon floss, built up, epoxied, pearl glitter optional on top
Eyes: Chartreuse prismatic stick-on, 3.5 mm

Notes: This is a great-looking baitfish pattern that gets results from persnickety pike. I fish this pattern in three color combinations, gray/white, chartreuse/white (given here), and one of my favorite pike-catching combinations, red/white, with white being the belly color.

Barry's Woolhead Pike Fly

This fly is a pure attractor pattern. By virtue of its long cylindrical shape, it is very suggestive of a number of prey fish. When I need a larger-than-normal offering, I'll throw this pattern. I use some silicone on the bottom of the wool head to help maintain its shape.

Icelandic sheep offers the illusion of bulk without adding a lot of weight, so I'm able to tie longer flies while keeping the weight manageable. Since this pattern is primarily used as a searching pattern, I opt for bright colors that can be seen from a distance.

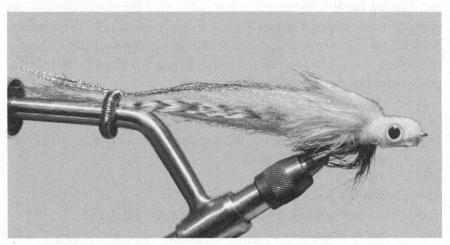

Barry's Woolhead Pike Fly

Recipe: Barry's Woolhead Pike Fly

Hook: Straight eye, extra strong, standard length, forged, stainless, e.g. Tiemco TMC 811S

Size: 3/0-5/0

Thread: Chartreuse single-strand nylon floss

Tail: Chartreuse Icelandic sheep, pearl Krystal Flash, one barred chartreuse saddle feather on each side

Collar: Chartreuse marabou

Head: Chartreuse ram's wool, spun, clipped to shape, with a light coating of silicone on the underside

Eyes: Chartreuse molded plastic eyes, 2.5 mm, glued in place with Zap-A-Gap (Super Glue)

Notes: My most productive colors have been all-chartreuse (given here) and a red/white combination where the tail is white and the head is red ram's wool with white silicone applied to the underside. I usually fish this pattern with a five-foot mini-sink-tip line to keep the fly at the depth I want.

Icelandic Pike Fly

Icelandic Pike Fly

This rather simple pattern relies on its seductive movement to catch fish. The long, stringy Icelandic sheep fibers undulate as the fly is being stripped. When adorned with Flashabou, it makes for an extremely effective attractor pattern. It can be tied in large sizes while maintaining ease of casting.

The Icelandic Pike Fly is easy to tie. More importantly, it catches pike on a regular basis. If you choose, you can add eyes to the head to give it a more fishy appearance before epoxy is applied. I urge you to tie and fish this pattern. In an age where we tend to lean on more complicated things to prove our worth, it's nice to see something so simple be so effective.

Recipe: Icelandic Pike Fly

Hook: Straight eye, extra strong, standard length, forged, stainless, e.g. Tiemco TMC 811S
Size: 3/0–5/0
Thread: Chartreuse single-strand nylon floss
Tail: Chartreuse Icelandic sheep, pearl Flashabou
Collar: Chartreuse Icelandic sheep, pearl Flashabou
Eyes: Chartreuse plastic molded, 2.5 mm
Head: Chartreuse single-strand nylon floss, built up, epoxied

Notes: I like to tie this pattern in typical pike-attracting colors like red-over-white, red-over-yellow, white, black, and the chartreuse pattern given here. The more action I can create with my retrieve, the more productive this pattern is.

Blanton's Flashtail Whistler

Blanton's Flashtail Whistler

This pattern has quickly become one of my favorites. It excels when pike are holding in a little deeper water that is slightly off-color. Flashtail Whistlers are often tied weighted to get the fly down to the fish. Whistlers attract by action, color, and flash, the three key ingredients of a successful attractor pattern. The shape appears to imitate nothing in particular, but when it's wet, this fly takes on a more fishy appearance.

Recipe: Blanton's Flashtail Whistler

Hook: Straight eye, heavy wire, semi-dropped point, forged, stainless, e.g. Tiemco TMC 800S
Size: 3/0
Thread: Red single-strand nylon floss
Tail: Yellow bucktail, silver Flashabou, rainbow Krystal Flash, grizzly neck hackles
Body: Red chenille
Collar: Large, webby red saddle hackle

Eyes: Large silver bead chain
Head: Red single-strand nylon floss, built up, epoxied

Notes: I fish the Whistler in bright colors for best results. Color schemes include all-white, a red collar with a yellow tail (given here), a red collar with a white tail, and a chartreuse collar with an orange tail. I've tried this pattern in all these colors, but red/yellow produces the best results. Also worth trying are the Blanton's Punch series of flies, which are similar but slimmer in profile.

Clouser's Half-and-Half

Clouser's Half-and-Half

Here's a hybrid that combines features from two of the most successful patterns ever created, the Clouser Minnow and Lefty's Deceiver. Bob Clouser and Lefty Kreh put their heads and their flies together to create a fly that can't miss. The Half-and-Half is an excellent choice for probing the water column.

This is the best deep-water fly to use when those miserable late spring storms throw a monkey wrench into the post-spawn fishing and push the pike deep. I have fished this pattern with floating, sink-tip, and full-sink lines with good results in each case. Whether I'm fishing spring, summer, or fall, I make sure I have a good supply of these flies. The Half-and-Half is an invaluable tool in my day-to-day pursuit of pike on the fly.

Recipe: Clouser's Half-and-Half

Hook: Straight eye, extra strong, standard length, forged, stainless,
           e.g. Tiemco TMC 811S
Size: 1/0-3/0
Thread: White 6/0
Tail: Six white saddle hackles, silver Flashabou
Collar: Red bucktail
Top: Red bucktail
Bottom: White bucktail
Eyes: Dumbbell eyes, red with black pupil
Head: White 6/0 thread, epoxied

Notes: The most productive color combinations are red/white (given here), chartreuse/orange/white, and all-white. This fly is tied and rides in the water with the hook up.

Popovic's Jiggy Fly

Popovic's Jiggy Fly

This fly is similar in function and fish-taking ability to the Clouser. It has a slim baitfish profile and can effectively be fished throughout the water column. It's particularly useful when you're trying to reach suspended pike or pike feeding near the bottom.

Fished with a floating line, the fly can be presented vertically much like a conventional angler would present a jig. While this presentation works in shallow water, it's necessary to use a sink-tip or full-sink line for deeper water.

The Jiggy uses a cone head instead of dumbbell eyes. The simple body is made of either bucktail or Ultra Hair, but it can be tied with feathers or rabbit strips for more action. Flash is also used, and the amount of flash you'll need is dependent on the water clarity and depths you're fishing. Most strikes with this type of fly occur on the fall, so be prepared and keep a tight line for constant contact on the way down.

Recipe: Popovic's Jiggy Fly

Hook: Straight eye, 3X strong, 4X long, forged, stainless, e.g. Tiemco TMC 911S
Size: 2-2/0
Thread: Fine monofilament thread
Body: Chartreuse over white bucktail or Ultra Hair, pearl Krystal Flash
Eyes: Orange prismatic stick-on, 2.5 mm
Head: Silver cone

Notes: Popovic also offers other versions of his highly successful Candy series of flies that work equally well. They are available with different types of weighted beads and cones. You can tie your own in pike-catching colors like red-over-white.

Popovic's 3D Baitfish

This is another brilliant streamer by outstanding fly designer Bob Popovic! The 3D Baitfish can be trimmed and shaped to match any food fish that swims, and the length and colors can be adjusted to mimic the naturals in your area. Even in very large sizes, these flies are very light and easy to cast, because the synthetic Ultra Hair doesn't absorb water. This is one of my favorite streamer patterns to throw when big pike are on the feed.

Recipe: Popovic's 3D Baitfish

Hook: Straight eye, extra strong, standard length, forged, stainless, e.g. Tiemco TMC 811S

Size: 2/0-4/0

Thread: Fine monofilament

Tail: White Ultra Hair or Super Hair, pearl Polar Flash

Body: Gary Ultra Hair or Super Hair, pearl Polar Flash

Head: Gray Ultra Hair or Super Hair, pearl Polar Flash

Eyes: Silver prismatic stick-on, 3.5 mm

Notes: Study the overall profile of the fish you're trying to imitate and take great care in trimming and shaping the fly. I've done well with red/white combinations and the standard gray/white (given here). Whatever combination you tie, remember to use lighter colors for the belly.

Divers

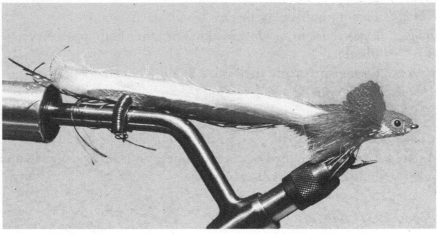

Dahlberg Rabbit-Strip Diver

Dahlberg Rabbit-Strip Diver

Without question, this is one of the most versatile flies in my arsenal. The Dahlberg Diver can be fished effectively throughout the water column. It's as much at home being popped through shallow water as it is being fished to suspended pike in eight feet of water. Wherever you find pike, you'll find a way to fish divers.

Extremely lightweight, Dahlberg Divers are easily cast all day long without arm fatigue. The one drawback to any fly constructed from deer hair is durability, but I'm willing to overlook that problem due to the effectiveness of these flies. They can be tied with a variety of tail materials and in any color to cover the range from imitations to attractor patterns.

Recipe: Dahlberg Rabbit-Strip Diver

Hook: Straight eye, extra strong, standard length, forged, stainless, e.g. Tiemco TMC 811S
Size: 1/0-3/0
Thread: White 3/0
Tail: 5□ white rabbit strip, red Flashabou
Collar: Red deer hair
Head: Red deer hair, white deer hair, stacked and spun with the white underneath, clipped to shape
Eyes: Yellow solid plastic, 3 mm
Weed Guard (optional): Mason hard mono, 25 lb.

Notes: To increase durability, use liberal amounts of Flexament during the tying process, and then apply more cement to the underside of the finished fly. During the spinning and clipping of the deer hair, take care in shaping the fly, making certain that the head is centered properly on the hook and the bottom is cut flat, so the fly floats, tracks, and dives properly.

Umpqua Pike Fly

This slightly bulkier version of the Dahlberg Diver uses a combination of tail materials that includes Icelandic sheep, saddle feathers, Flashabou, and Krystal Flash. These materials come alive when stripped through water and offer a slightly larger profile than the Dahlberg's rabbit-strip tail.

The only real downfall to this fly is that unless you tie your own, you have only one choice of color, chartreuse/frog (given here). If you tie, I suggest trying an all-white version or a red/white combination. I use this fly instead of the standard diver for the times when pike are looking for a larger meal. Due to the bulkier head design, the fly does not dive as deep, so if you're trying to reach deeper water, a medium-length sink-tip or a full-sink line will help.

Umpqua Pike Fly

Recipe: Umpqua Pike Fly

Hook: Straight eye, extra strong, standard length, forged, stainless, e.g. Tiemco TMC 811S

Size: 1/0-3/0

Thread: Chartreuse single-strand nylon floss

Tail: Chartreuse Icelandic sheep, yellow, chartreuse-barred, and red saddle hackles, chartreuse Krystal Flash, saltwater pearl Flashabou

Collar: Chartreuse and black deer hair, spun, flared

Head: Chartreuse, black, and white deer hair, spun, clipped to shape

Eyes: Yellow molded plastic, 3.5 mm

Weed Guard (optional): Mason hard mono, 25 lb.

Notes: Great care should be taken in shaping the head and diving collar on all divers using clipped deer hair, as one wrong snip can ruin the fly. Trim the bottom as flat and evenly as possible to ensure the fly sits upright on the water, allowing it to dive properly. It's always a good idea to carry scissors with you on the water, so you can adjust the trim if necessary.

Umpqua Swimming Baitfish

Umpqua Swimming Baitfish

The Umpqua Swimming Baitfish offers a flatter, broader head than other divers, while incorporating a shorter diving collar. This combination creates a fly that dives and runs considerably closer to the surface. When fished with short, consistent strips, it gives the appearance of a baitfish darting around the surface, an action that proves irresistible.

This fly, used with a sink-tip line, is my favorite combo for taking suspended tiger muskies from local lakes. This pattern always moves well-educated fish that get heavy fishing pressure and have seen every presentation—both fly and conventional. It typically hooks a few, as well. On my local pike water, I have great success with this fly on super-smart pike when nothing else works.

Recipe: Umpqua Swimming Baitfish

Hook: Straight eye, extra strong, standard length, forged, stainless, e.g. Tiemco TMC 811S
Size: 1/0-3/0
Thread: Red 3/0

Tail: 4 white saddle hackles outside, 2 grizzly saddle hackles
         inside, pearl Krystal Flash
Throat: Red Krystal Flash
Body: White rabbit, white hackle
Collar: Natural deer hair, flared
Head: White, orange, and red deer hair, spun
Eyes: Gold molded plastic, 2.5 mm
Weed Guard (optional): Mason hard mono, 25 lb.

Notes: I stick with natural colors for this diver, trying to mimic local baitfish, such as shad. Other colors worth trying are red/yellow and red/white.

Umpqua Swimming Waterdog

Umpqua Swimming Waterdog

This is another excellent pattern created by one of flyfishing's greats, Dave Whitlock. This fly imitates the nymph or gilled stage of the tiger salamander, a favorite on the pike's menu. Tied in black, with highlights of yellow and chartreuse, it closely resembles the real thing.

This pattern is most effective when fished around vegetation or other forms of cover. It's tied with a diving collar, and when fished with a sink-tip or full-sink line using the stop-and-go retrieve, this pattern can be deadly on big pike.

Recipe: Umpqua Swimming Waterdog

Hook: Bass bug, straight eye, fine wire, wide gape, forged, bronze,
e.g. Tiemco TMC 8089

Size: 2

Thread: Chartreuse single-strand nylon floss

Tail: 6□ black rabbit strip, 1□ section of chartreuse rabbit (glued
to underside), chartreuse Krystal Flash, chartreuse-dyed
grizzly hackle

Collar: Black deer hair

Head: Black deer hair, spun, clipped to shape

Legs: Black round rubber strands, chartreuse round rubber
strands

Eyes: Yellow molded plastic, 3 mm

Weed Guard: Mason hard mono, 25 lb.

Notes: I've tried other colors, including white and red/white, with
some success, but the black pattern given here mimics the natural best.

Stewart's Snook-A-Roo

Stewart's Snook-A-Roo

I knew this fly was a must the first time I saw it. Originally designed
for snook, this fly offers the more compact, yet beefier profile I like to
present to pike when I'm getting lots of close follows but no takes.

When this happens, I can usually switch down in size, change to this pattern, and convert many of those frustrating follows into takes.

When fished on a floating line, the Snook-A-Roo is more of a waking fly that travels just below the surface, waking water over its top behind a steady, smooth retrieve. Presented with a sink-tip or full-sink line, the fly fishes and acts more like a diver. Again, I offer this bit of advice. When you're getting lots of follows, try switching the size, shape, and action of your fly. Your hook-up ratio will increase dramatically.

Recipe: Stewart's Snook-A-Roo

Hook: Straight eye, extra strong, standard length, forged, stainless, e.g. Tiemco TMC 811S
Size: 1/0-3/0
Thread: Fluorescent fire-orange single-strand nylon floss
Tail: White bucktail, grizzly hackles, pearl Flashabou, pearl Krystal Flash, red marabou
Butt: Red chenille
Collar: White deer hair, flared
Head: White, natural, and black deer hair, spun
Eyes: Blue molded plastic, 9 mm
Weed Guard (optional): Mason hard mono, 25 lb.

Notes: The pattern given here is the original version— white with a touch of black blended in on top and red marabou tied in for color on the tail. I've found no need to change colors, but you can experiment with colors to find your own favorite.

Whitlock Waker Shad Fly

Master angler and ever-creative fly tier Dave Whitlock designed this very effective fly. The Waker Fly is another deer-hair baitfish pattern that can be used to imitate anything from shad to bluegill when tied in the appropriate colors. It has a broad head, and when fished just below the surface, it creates a small wake, much like nervous baitfish do— just before they're eaten.

The Waker Fly is most effective when fished near the surface, and because of this, you might expect a floating line to be best for the job.

The problem with floating lines is that they also create a wake that can distract from the fly. It's better to use an intermediate line, if you have one, so that the water in front of the fly remains calm and the pike's attention is drawn toward the waking fly.

Whitlock Waker Shad Fly

Recipe: Whitlock Waker Shad Fly

Hook:　Bass bug, straight eye, fine wire, wide gape, forged, nickel plated, e.g. Tiemco TMC 8089NP

Size:　2

Thread: White 3/0

Tail:　Gray and white Icelandic sheep, pearl Krystal Flash, pearl Flashabou, saltwater pearl Flashabou, gray neck hackle

Gills:　Red Synthetic Living Fiber gill dubbing

Head:　Light gray, dark gray, and white deer hair, spun, clipped to shape

Eyes:　Silver 3-D molded, 3 mm

Weed Guard (optional): Mason hard mono, 25 lb.

Notes: The three original versions of this pattern were tied in colors to suggest shad (given here), bluegill, and golden shiner. I've experimented with other colors, including red with a white belly and all-chartreuse, as well, and have experienced great success.

Tinker Mackerel

Tinker Mackerel

Here's one more fly from the saltwater side that has been an outstanding big-pike fly when tied in the right colors. This large, bulky fly offers even the largest of pike a sizable meal. Although it's tied with a deer-hair head, the Tinker Mackerel really doesn't fall into the diver category or the waker category, but instead fills its own niche somewhere in between.

I like to fish the Tinker Mackerel with a sink-tip line over and around submerged cover. This fly fishes extremely well in the neutral-density presentation, because it hangs seductively in the water column. It has accounted for many big pike and muskies for me.

Recipe: Tinker Mackerel

Hook: Straight eye, heavy wire, semi-dropped point, forged, stainless, e.g. Tiemco TMC 800S
Size: 2/0-4/0
Thread: White single-strand nylon floss
Tail: Aqua, light blue, and grizzly saddle hackles, circled with aqua, light blue, white, and pink marabou
Collar: Lavender deer hair, flared
Head: Lavender, light blue, blue-gray, and green deer hair, spun, clipped to shape
Eyes: Amber molded plastic, 3.5 mm

Notes: The original pattern (given here) uses colors to imitate a mackerel, but I also use colors to match local forage. I always carry a few of these patterns tied in red-and-white, too. When big fish are on the prowl for a substantial meal at medium depths, it's time to break out the Tinker Mackerel.

Popovic's Pop-Lip Full Dress

This ingenious design is the product of innovative fly designer Bob Popovic. The Pop-Lip Fly utilizes a diving lip that not only causes the fly to dive but also creates side-to-side movement. The actions of this fly are very similar to those of the short-lipped, diving crank baits used by conventional anglers.

Bob strongly recommends the use of a two-hand retrieve in order to get the best movement from this fly. Place the rod under your casting arm and use both hands to retrieve the fly and maintain the constant speed necessary to create the action that makes the fly so deadly.

The colors may be altered to match the local forage base, or you may elect to use bright, flashy colors to make the Pop-Lip an attractor pattern. This is a fly I use when fishing to pike that experience extreme pressure. Many times the only thing it takes to get these fish to take a fly is to show them something they haven't seen. I like fishing the Pop-Lip near the surface with a floating line, as well as with a sink-tip line to cover the water column, much as I do with deer-hair divers.

Recipe: Popovic's Pop-Lip Full Dress

Hook: Straight eye, extra strong, standard length, forged, stainless, e.g. Tiemco TMC 811S
Size: 3/0
Thread: Fine monofilament thread
Tail: White bucktail, yellow ostrich herl, yellow saddle hackles
Head: Yellow and white sheep fleece or ram's wool, spun, trimmed, coated with silicone
Diving lip: White sheep fleece or ram's wool teased out from head, trimmed, coated with silicone
Eyes: Orange prismatic stick-on, 3.5 mm

Notes: Bob suggests leaving the lip a little long until the fly can be tested in the water. The diving lip can then be trimmed so the correct action is created.

Popovic's Siliclone Fly

By using ram's wool and silicone, this popular fly can be shaped to represent many baitfish. Almost any shape can be achieved, from round to oval and from flat to fat. The Siliclone Fly is part popper and part waking fly. Fished with short, jerky retrieves, it acts much like a popper. Longer, more constant retrieves create waking that can be very effective.

When fished behind a sinking line, this fly fits well into my neutral-density presentations. The silicone creates a protective barrier between the water and the wool that helps the fly float. By holding the fly underwater and gently squeezing and releasing the head, the fly will absorb water, creating a neutral-buoyancy fly. The silicone also makes for a more durable fly. Flies that do become damaged can easily be repaired later by reapplying silicone back at your fly-tying desk.

Recipe: Popovic's Siliclone Fly

Hook: Straight eye, heavy wire, semi-dropped point, forged, stainless, e.g. Tiemco TMC 800S
Size: 1/0-3/0
Thread: Fine monofilament thread
Tail: White bucktail, white ostrich herl, pearl Flashabou
Head: Chartreuse sheep fleece or ram's wool, trimmed to shape, coated with silicone
Eyes: Silver prismatic stick-on, 3.5 mm

Notes: I also have great success with this pattern in solid colors. My favorite colors so far are yellow and white.

Poppers

Popovic's Banger

This saltwater popper is a large-profile noisemaker that draws lots of attention when pike are feeding near the surface or are holding in shallow water. Popovic's Banger is tied with a Live Body foam cylinder, making it quite durable. The Banger floats extremely well and won't soak up water like deer-hair poppers.

This fly floats high, and when I'm looking to make a bang, I fish it with a sink-tip line to really cause a ruckus. This is a great combo technique for fishing dirty water and also for fishing in and around large cabbage beds where I want the fly to make as much noise as possible, notifying all fish in the immediate vicinity of the fly's presence.

Popovic's Banger

Recipe: Popovic's Banger

Hook: Straight eye, 3X strong, 4X long, forged, stainless, e.g.
Tiemco TMC 911S
Size: 1/0-4/0
Thread: White Gudebrod size D rod-wrapping thread
Tail: Chartreuse bucktail
Body: Chartreuse pearl Estaz
Head: Live Body foam cylinder wrapped with chartreuse prismatic tape
Eyes: Large silver prismatic stick-on

Notes: The materials necessary to make this fly are available in all the colors of the rainbow, so your imagination is your only limitation.

I personally have done well with an all-white version, but that doesn't mean I haven't had fun experimenting.

Stewart's Dancing Frog

Stewart's Dancing Frog

Here is an innovative pattern from deer-hair artist Jim Stewart. Jim took the ever-popular Hula Popper and made a replica using deer hair. This popper-style fly uses a broad, flat face to create major water displacement as it's jerked and ripped back through the water. Some of the most violent strikes I've had have been on this fly. Probably the hardest thing to do when you get a strike like that is to react to the feeling of the weight of the fish and not the water erupting in your face.

Depending on its color scheme, this fly can imitate an injured baitfish flopping along the surface or a frog kicking its way through some lily pads! When I'm looking for a little extra noise or surface disturbance, I fish this fly behind a short, five-foot sink-tip for that extra pop.

Recipe: Stewart's Dancing Frog

Hook: Bass bug, straight eye, fine wire, wide gape, forged, nickel plated, e.g. Tiemco TMC 8089NP
Size: 2-1/0
Thread: Chartreuse single-strand nylon floss
Tail: Chartreuse rubber strands, yellow rubber strands

Body: Chartreuse, olive, black, and dark green deer hair stacked
over yellow, clipped to shape
Eyes: Orange molded plastic, 3.5 mm
Weed Guard: Mason hard mono, 25 lb., double-looped

Notes: With its double-loop weed guard, this fly can be fished in heavy
vegetation. The colors of the versions I typically fish include frog
(given here), gray-over-white, and red-over-white.

Stewart's Lucky Wiggler

Stewart's Lucky Wiggler

This great little pattern packs a big punch. The unique, short, tightly
clipped, deer-hair nose quickly gives way to a tall, blunt collar that
helps push this fly slightly subsurface and creates a distinct side-to-
side wiggle. The action of this fly is a real fish attractor. When fished
properly, it brings even the biggest pike to the surface to investigate.

This fly is just plain fun to fish! I enjoy and look forward to the
times I can fish it, as I experiment with different retrieves. My best
presentation and retrieve combination includes the use of a short, five-
foot sink-tip line that aides in forcing the fly below the surface. My retrieve then involves a two-handed strip retrieve to keep the fly moving
steadily while creating that fish-enticing wiggle.

Recipe: Stewart's Lucky Wiggler

Hook: Bass bug, straight eye, fine wire, wide gape, forged, nickel
          plated, e.g. Tiemco TMC 8089NP
Size: 2-1/0
Thread: Red single-strand nylon floss
Tail: White rubber strands, six grizzly hackles, silver Flashabou,
          red Krystal Flash
Butt: Fluorescent red chenille
Head: White, natural, black, and red deer hair, spun, clipped to
          shape
Eyes: White plastic molded, 3 mm
Weed guard: Mason hard mono, 25 lb.

Notes: I have to be honest here—while I have the tying ability and have tied each and every pattern listed in this section, this is one of the many patterns using clipped deer hair that I prefer to purchase. This pattern, while fun to tie, takes a lot of time to create, and the deer hair must be trimmed precisely to make the fly run true. I tie my streamers and purchase these more elaborate patterns, trying to balance my time and my money.

Mouserat

When mice are on the menu and pike are feeding near the surface, this can be the most unnerving pattern to fish. The strikes produced by mouse patterns are the ones you heard me talk about, the ones where grown men drop their rods and run for shore. It can truly be eye-opening and heart-stopping when pike hit these flies. Maybe you've seen great white sharks attack seals on The Discovery Channel?

My first experience with mouse patterns came while I was fishing for large rainbow trout on the Alagnak River in Alaska. My guide asked me if I'd ever skated mice for trout. After a brief explanation, I asked to see this tactic in action. Then I tried it myself. I took several nice double-digit rainbows, and I was in awe of the spectacular takes. My guide said, "If you think this is cool, you should see what pike in the sloughs do to mouse patterns."

I had to see this! We moved to a shallow slough off the river. Instead of letting me cast right away, my guide walked through the heavy brush and spooked a couple of mice into the water. They began to swim frantically to the opposite shoreline, and all hell broke loose. In mere seconds both mice had disappeared. As the water calmed, I cast, and my presentation was met with an immediate, the-world-is-coming-to-an-end take. I was hooked. And so was the pike.

Mouserat

Recipe: Mouserat

Hook: Bass bug, straight eye, fine wire, wide gape, forged, nickel plated, e.g. Tiemco TMC 8089NP
Size: 2-6
Thread: Tan 3/0
Tail: Tan chamois
Body: Natural deer hair, left long on top with bottom trimmed flat
Ears: Tan chamois
Head: Natural deer hair, spun, clipped to shape
Whiskers: Black moose
Eyes: Black Pantone pen
Weed guard: Mason hard mono, 25 lb.

Notes: This pattern is also available in all-black. There are assorted versions, including one that has a deer-hair head and a body that is nothing more than root-beer-colored Flashabou that also fishes well. The pattern given here, however, is the most realistic. We are, after all, trying to match the hatch.

Blado's Crease Fly

Blado's Crease Fly

This ingenious pattern was developed by Captain Joe Blado for East Coast saltwater fishing. Even though it was originally developed for the salt, this pattern excels at taking freshwater species that feed on other fish. My first experience with this pattern was while fishing for peacock bass in Brazil. With the success I experienced there, I just knew it would work for taking northern pike feeding on or near the surface.

Not really a popper nor a streamer, this pattern crosses the threshold and can be successfully fished either way. On the surface, with a floating line, where erratic retrieves bring violent strikes, the Crease Fly is quite popper-like. It can also be fished effectively subsurface with a sink-tip or full-sink line. Fished like a streamer, it behaves very much like an erratic baitfish. Make sure you add this excellent crossover pattern to your pike arsenal before your next outing.

Recipe: Blado's Crease Fly

Hook: Straight eye, extra strong, 3X long, forged, stainless, e.g.
Tiemco TMC 911S
Size: 1/0-3/0
Thread: White single-strand nylon floss
Tail: White, brown, and black bucktail, pearl Krystal Flash, gold
Flashabou
Body: White craft foam (adhesive back), pearl Mylar foil, colored
with Pantone pen, coated with epoxy
Eyes: Silver prismatic stick-on, 3.5 mm

Notes: You have several options when it comes to this pattern. For those who really enjoy their fly tying and have a creative side, the Mylar foil comes in an almost infinite color selection with different background schemes. It also will take color markers such as Pantone pens, allowing you to add bars, spots, and different colors. For the less adventurous, you can buy kits that come with everything you need, pre-cut and ready to tie. Of course, you can purchase the fly from your local shop, but your color selection will be limited. Whatever you decide to do, make sure you have some with you the next time you venture out.

Overview

As you can see, there are many patterns available to the pike fly angler. Poppers, sliders, wakers, divers, streamers—they all can be tied in a variety of ways to suggest naturals or simply to get the pike's attention. When combined with what you learned in the presentation chapter, these patterns should give you the basis to go out and experience success in most situations.

Don't be afraid to alter patterns and come up with your own ideas or color schemes. They might work better for you in your local waters. What I've given you here is a guide to some of the more popular and productive patterns, but it is in no way an exhaustive list of the many patterns available. Experimentation fosters ingenuity, so use your imagination and be creative.

SEVEN

FLY TACKLE FOR PIKE

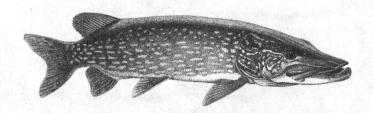

Flyfishing for pike, as with any other target species, requires specialized tackle. You don't want to go to a gunfight armed with a knife. Those of you reading this book are obviously serious pike flyfishers, and you need appropriate tools. These tools range from rods capable of throwing large, wind-resistant flies to hook-outs that allow safe removal of those flies from jaws filled with razor-sharp teeth. Other specialized items include jaw spreaders and steel leaders.

If you chase pike throughout the season, you must be able to cover the water from top to bottom. Your selection of fly lines will need to include floating, sink-tip, and full-sink lines. You've also seen how an inexpensive thermometer can help immensely in identifying appropriate water temperatures. These are the tools of the trade, and while some might seem rather simplistic at first, they are all vital to your ultimate success.

In this chapter, I'll take a closer look at the tackle and associated tools most often found in my possession when I'm pursuing pike. While I will mention the brands I'm most familiar with and use regularly, that doesn't mean there aren't fine products offered by other manufacturers. With that in mind, let's take a look inside the pike flyfisher's gear bag.

Rods for Pike

I like to have a different rod for each situation I may face. On a trip to Manitoba, Canada to film a video, this fact drew a lot of attention. It was a twenty-day trip, and I took several rods—twelve to be exact.

I like to have a different rod for each situation I may face.

The Canadian customs agent asked me why I had so many rods. After giving several fruitless answers, I politely asked her if she played golf.

"Yes," she answered. "Why do you ask?"

"Do you play with only one club?"

She handed the rod case back to me and said, "Next!"

Flyfishing for pike has become a deep, driving passion for me. Dedicated trout flyfishermen have a rod for every situation—one for nymph fishing, another for dry flies, and another one for flyfishing stillwaters. Serious pike anglers, or at least those with a budget to do so, collect just as many, if not more, rods in assorted sizes for specific situations.

As an example, I prefer eight-weight rods for casting deer-hair divers and poppers. When throwing larger-than-normal flies and using full-sink lines, a ten-weight rod serves me better. If you're on a budget and need to buy just one rod, split the difference and go with a nine-weight, which handles each of those situations pretty well. If I were forced to pack just one rod for a trip, I'd select a nine-weight, because of its versatility.

You can't go wrong with any of these three line weights, but I strongly urge you to try out rods on the water before selecting one.

Most quality fly shops offer demo models for customers to try before they buy. With the price of rods today, it's an investment that warrants some research.

Rod action is worth a brief discussion. As you know by now, pike can grow to large proportions, in excess of twenty pounds. In addition, you'll be throwing large, wind-resistant flies that may be larger than some of the trout you catch! Toss in the fact that many of these flies are made from materials that soak up enormous amounts of water, and casting can be difficult with a rod that's not designed to do what you're asking it to do. Make sure your rod is one that can handle the task.

Saltwater rods are a good choice. They're designed to handle similar elements—big water, strong winds, and powerful fish. They also make casting large pike flies somewhat tolerable, maybe even enjoyable. Sinking lines and weighted flies are no problem, since these rods are specifically designed with them in mind. Most of today's saltwater rods also come with a fighting butt, which will help you by providing extra leverage and something more comfortable to place against your side while fighting big fish.

Rod length is often the topic of great debates. For many years, long rods were almost trendy, and shorter rods lost some of their popularity. But flyfishing for pike isn't about fashion. My personal preference is for shorter rods (eight-and-a-half feet) when I'm casting to specific fish and accuracy is important due to tight cover. Longer rods (nine to ten feet) are my preference when fishing more open water where long casts become important. Longer rods also serve you better when wade fishing or belly-boating. The extra length will help your backcast immensely.

Multiple-piece rods have become quite popular with today's flyfishers, who often travel globally. Early multi-piece rods were stiffer and heavier than their two-piece counterparts, making them less desirable. With the current ferrule technology, today's three- to five-piece rods are only slightly heavier, and their flex patterns are very similar to two-piece rods. While more expensive, they're worth the price, especially if you plan on doing any travel that involves airplanes.

With all that said, what do I use? I prefer the Sage Rod RPLXiII saltwater series. I've used Sage since the very beginning and have found no reason to change. When I travel to pike destinations, my rod case contains one 886-3 RPLXiII rod, two 990-3 RPLXiII rods, and one 1090-3 RPLXiII rod. The first figure in the model number represents the line weight, the next two numbers represent rod length, and the last number represents the number of pieces. Of course, I encourage you try the rods of other quality manufacturers and make a choice based on your own preferences.

Reels for Pike

Your choice of a reel should take into consideration the other types of flyfishing you might be doing. Pike are notorious more for their strike than their stamina in a fight. In more than twenty years of chasing pike with a fly, I've only had four pike take me into my backing. Instead of prolonged fights, expect vicious strikes, quick bursts of speed, and short runs. Most pike fights are short-lived and done at close quarters; they rarely require lots of backing.

If you're anything like me and have the urge to explore all species that readily eat a fly, you'll want to think about what you need in a reel for those other species. For example, if you're going to be doing some saltwater or salmon fishing, you'll want to look at a reel that is up to the task of controlling long, fast runs that often go into the backing. That reel can double as your pike reel.

Reels with a good, modern drag system offer many advantages over older reels. These reels give you the ability to fight the fish with your reel as well as with your rod. By using the reel's drag system, I'm able to apply extra pressure to the fish and control those bursts of speed for which pike are so famous. Applying drag resistance on the reel prevents overruns and the resulting bird's nest. Reels with exposed rims offer the added advantage of allowing you to apply pressure with your palm and slow the fish as needed. One word of caution here, though. The pike flyfisherman must be careful of knuckle-busting runs—truly knuckle busting!

Other considerations worth noting include choosing a reel of the proper weight to balance the rod and reduce arm fatigue. Quick-release spools that make switching from one line to another painless, easy, and fast are essential. The finish is important, too. I'm not talking about how nice your reel looks brand new, but how well it will stand up to harsh elements. Anodized finishes protect reels from the rigors of saltwater fishing. They will last for years, as long as the reels are rinsed with freshwater and cleaned and lubed on a regular basis. I also have a preference for today's large-arbor designs that allow quicker line retrieval.

Last, but not least, is price. Today's modern reels average from $200 to $400, with some reels approaching $800. My personal preference for a high-quality reel in the midlevel price range is Ross Reels. I've used Ross Reels for years, and they have performed flawlessly under every possible condition. Whether I'm pike fishing or chasing peacock bass in Brazil, the Ross Big Game Series reel is my model of choice. As with rods, there are many other fine manufacturers of quality reels that are more than capable of handling the job. Your needs, personal preference, and budget will help make your final decision.

Fly Lines for Pike

As you know, flyfishing for pike throughout the season requires that you have the ability to cover the water from top to bottom. Floating lines, sink-tips, and full-sink lines will all be part of your arsenal. Your lines must be capable of turning over large, bushy flies—even in the face of the stiffest winds. There are many fine lines on the shelves today, so where should you start? Let's begin at the top and work to the bottom.

Floating lines come in many sizes, colors, and tapers. Many of today's manufacturers even offer species-specific lines. Rio, Scientific Anglers, and Cortland all offer specialty lines for pike. These lines are exaggerated weight-forward lines with a radically short front taper and an oversized belly. The lines have a short rear taper with a small-diameter running line behind. This design allows for easy fly turnover and provides enough weight to punch big flies through the toughest winds.

Casting these specialty lines requires some practice. Most people try to carry too much line in the air. By doing so, they overload the rod and kill the cast. It's better to carry twenty to twenty-five feet of line in the air with another twenty to twenty-five feet off at your side. Shoot the remaining line, much the way you would with a shooting-head system. Before you go out fishing, visit a park and practice casting your new pike line. After you've become accustomed to how it handles,

Your lines must be capable of turning over large, bushy flies—even in the stiffest winds.

you'll be quite comfortable with it. A specialty line for pike is well worth the investment.

There are lots of decisions to make in choosing a sink-tip line. The sinking portion of the line can range from five feet to twenty feet or more in length. Sink-tip lines are offered with different sink rates designed to cover shallow to mid-depths. For almost all pike applications, shorter tips, five to twelve feet in length, will serve you best. Long sink-tips are of little use for presentations at the depths you'll usually fish. I avoid tips that are longer than the depth of water I'm fishing, and most pike fishing is done in relatively shallow water.

I most commonly use sink-tip lines in shallow to mid-depth water for presentations to fish suspended over cabbage beds or some other form of cover. I also use them when I'm probing edges where deep water meets the shallows. I throw every type of fly in combination with sink-tip lines to cover that water at a variety of depths and angles, as you know from the presentations chapter.

Rio's "density-compensated" sink-tips in seven-foot and fifteen-foot lengths are a favorite of mine. These lines are designed with a balanced floating body that reduces the hinging effect during the casting stroke that is common to many sink-tip and full-sink lines. Additionally, the density compensation allows the tip of the line to sink first, which prevents the curving effect common to many lines. The end result is a line that provides more accurate depth control. Better strike detection is also possible with this more precise line performance.

While I prefer a type 3 or type 4 sink rate for my pike fishing, there are many sink rates available. Water depths primarily determine the sink rate you need. Rio offers their density-compensated tips in several sink rates: type 3 with a sink rate of two to three inches per second and an effective fishing depth of two to five feet, type 4 with a sink rate of four to five inches per second and a depth of three to seven feet, type 6 with a sink rate of six to seven inches per second and a depth of eight to fifteen feet, and type 8 with a sink rate of eight to nine inches per second and an effective fishing depth of fifteen feet or more. By matching your sink rate to the depth of water you're fishing, you'll be able to keep your fly in the strike zone longer, making you a much more efficient angler.

When pike are holding tight to bottom structure and are reluctant to move far, a full-sink line may be required to reach them. Use of a full-sink line is my last choice. To be quite honest with you, I hate to cast one for long periods of time. The weight of a full-sink line combined with large, bulky flies simply makes casting this rig an unpleasant experience. With that said, full-sink lines do have their place and can save the day, particularly when pike are holding deep. The neutral-buoyancy technique that works so well for suspended, deep-water pike requires full-sink lines in combination with floating flies. This presentation can be deadly for even the most finicky of pike.

Full-sink lines come in sink rates similar to those of sink-tip lines, ranging from two inches per second to eight inches per second. I usually use one with a sink rate of six inches per second. These sink rates let you determine how deep you're presenting your fly and how quickly you're getting there. They also ensure that you keep your flies at the depth you want to fish. In the summer months or during springtime cold fronts when pike are forced deep, full-sink lines are worth their weight in gold. They allow you to get your fly to fish that would be out of reach otherwise. Poppers, divers, and streamers can all be effectively fished in combination with full-sink lines.

Each type of fly line serves a purpose, and you should have all three available when you head out flyfishing for pike. Lines are just as important as any other part of your equipment. Don't try to save money here! Cheap lines will crack and be short-lived. Spend the extra dollars on high-quality lines made by reputable manufacturers, and you won't have line problems on the water.

Leaders for Pike

During the early years, hard-monofilament leaders were favored by most of us who pursued pike on the fly. It wasn't that steel leaders weren't available, but the fact is they were just too difficult to work with. They were thick and almost cable-like in appearance. Tying knots was impossible; they kinked, coiled, and caused most presentations to look unnatural at best. Thank goodness for the continuing development of our industry. Improvements come each year in everything from rod designs to better leader systems.

Today's steel leaders are smaller in diameter and more flexible than those in use when I started flyfishing for pike. Many of these user-friendly leaders now allow you to tie knots in them. Gone are the outdated twist-melt methods and crimp sleeves, which we used to attach flies. Now you can tie flies directly to the steel. Companies such as Climax, American Wire, and Tyger Wire all offer superb steel-leader products.

Other manufacturers, such as Rio, Cortland, and Scientific Anglers, now offer pre-rigged steel leaders for pike. These leaders come in twenty- to thirty-pound test and seven- to nine-foot lengths. They come with crimp sleeves, but I immediately discard them, since they add more weight and commonly fail after prolonged use. Instead, I've found that the common jam knot (two overhand knots pulled against one another) works well for steel-leader-to-fly connections. This knot creates an open loop that allows more action from your fly and is quite simple to tie, even in the coldest weather.

For those who prefer to tie their own leaders, it's easily done with a length of hard monofilament and a short section of steel. Both Mason and Rio offer hard mono in spools of twenty-five yards, and Climax, American Wire, and Tyger Wire sell similar spools of steel leader. I

Today's steel leaders are smaller in diameter and more flexible.

fashion my pike leaders by starting with about six-and-a-half feet of twenty-two-pound hard mono and eighteen inches of twenty-pound steel. Keep in mind that if it's a world record you're after, there are specific requirements for leader setups that must be followed. Refer to the I.G.F.A. record book for exact specifications.

Your knot connections are critical, of course, to prevent weak spots in your leader system. The best knot for the mono-to-steel connection is the Albright. This knot surrounds and grips the steel, providing excellent strength. I use this knot exclusively, because the failure rate is extremely low. Incidentally, I don't tie my leaders using the tapered design typical of trout leaders. Instead I use a level leader, since delicate presentation is not an issue.

As I mentioned, I use a jam knot for my steel-to-fly connection. This simple knot is made with two overhand knots pulled or jammed against one another. To make this connection, start by tying one overhand knot in the steel leader near the tip, pull it down tight, and trim the tag. Roughly two inches behind this terminal knot, tie a second overhand knot. Don't pull it tight yet. Run the terminal knot through the eye of the fly and back through the open second overhand knot. (On smaller hooks, you may have to tie the second overhand knot first, run the steel through the eye, and then tie the terminal knot.) Now simply pull the second knot tight, closing the loop. The terminal knot will jam against the second. Simple, yet effective!

For my mono-to-fly-line connection, I use a loop-to-loop system. I put braided loops on the ends of my fly lines to make it convenient to remove and add leaders. At the end of the leader, I tie a perfection loop. I find this loop-to-loop connection clean, easy to use, and most importantly, strong. When I get lazy and don't feel like tying a perfection loop, I'll use a simple clinch knot. Three turns, back through the hole, and pull it down tight. Make sure to wet your knot before tightening to ensure it cinches properly. An improved clinch knot is difficult to tie with hard mono and is not necessary.

Organizing Your Pike Flies

Pike flies are so large and bulky that three pike flies would fill an entire trout fly box! So how do I store and transport my pike flies?

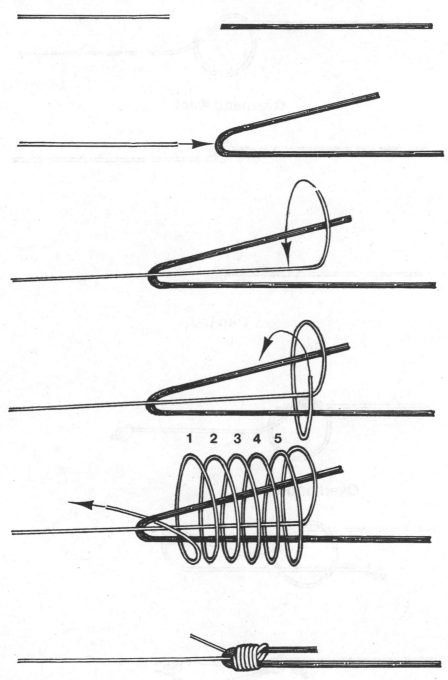

Albright knot

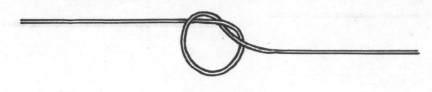

Overhand Knot

Trim tag

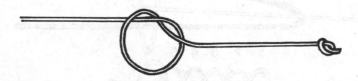

Overhand Knot

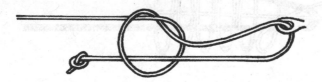

Jam knot

First, I purchase small Ziploc storage bags, two by six inches, from a local plastic bag company. I typically buy a few thousand of these at a time, enough to get me through several seasons. I place each of my flies in a bag to protect it from the elements until I'm ready to use it. When I'm out fishing, I carry a number of the flies I plan to use that day, in their bags, in my shirt or coat pocket.

While that system covers individual storage and on-the-water use, I also had to develop a way to store and organize large numbers of flies. I needed a system to transport large numbers of flies for trips and a way to sort through all those flies efficiently. I borrowed from the conventional side of angling here.

I use a soft-sided, three-ring binder system originally designed to hold plastic worms and spinner-baits. These binders are available from Cabela's and Bass Pro Shop. They cost $40 to $50 dollars, but they're a great way to store your flies. They'll also save you lots of frustration when you're searching for a specific fly.

The binders usually have about twelve large, tear-resistant Ziploc bags. Each of those bags accommodates a lot of flies. I sort my flies by types—streamers, divers, and poppers—and that makes finding a specific pattern much easier. The overall size of the binder is about ten by twelve inches, and it's about four to six inches thick. Although the binder is too big to carry in my vest, it's easily transported in my boat bag, where it provides easy access to individual flies when I need to grab a couple and throw them in my pocket.

Tools of the Trade

When you have over three feet of angry northern pike with a mouth full of razor-sharp teeth thrashing about, common sense dictates that you keep exposed fingers at a safe distance.

I once watched someone handling a pike who either didn't know any better or thought … well, let's face it, he just didn't think! Barehanded, without tools, he tried to remove a fly from a deeply hooked pike. If you've ever seen meat run through a grinder, you know what his fingers looked like when the pike was through with him. After thirty-two stitches, that angler now understands the importance of being properly equipped. And, no, it wasn't me!

So, first, jaw spreaders are a useful tool. Northern pike have a nasty habit of clamping down on something and not wanting to let go. Jaw spreaders are spring-loaded, heavy-gauge wire and must be used with great care in order not to harm the fish. They should not be used on small to medium-sized fish, since the jaw spreaders may be stronger than the pike's bite. A pair of needle-nosed pliers used in reverse is often all that's needed for smaller fish.

To use jaw spreaders properly, start by squeezing the jaw spreaders together in the middle section and inserting the tool into the pike's mouth. Slowly release the pressure. This tool holds the pike's mouth open so you can remove your fly safely, without fear of the pike chomping down on your fingers. One more word of caution. When you buy jaw spreaders, file off the sharp ends of the spreader's jaws. They usually come from the manufacturer that way, and the sharp ends can cause damage to the fish.

Your hook-set will dictate where in the pike's mouth your fly ends up. Strip-striking your fish before you lay into your hook-set will usually pull the fly toward the outer part of the mouth. This takes experience, and you won't always be able to control where the fly ends up. With some practice and patience, however, you may find you rarely need jaw-spreaders, except for the occasional fish that totally devours your fly while chasing it straight at you.

More important than jaw spreaders is another tool not normally associated with flyfishing—hook-outs. This tool is designed to reach and remove flies without putting your fingers in the pike's mouth. They are roughly ten inches long, with a small set of serrated jaws and a squeeze trigger to close the jaws and grab the fly. Long, needle-nosed pliers will work, but hook-outs are better suited for the job. Pinching down the barbs on your hooks greatly aids in releasing fish safely and quickly. Debarbed flies also reduce the damage that may be done to the fish during the fight and its subsequent release.

Since jaw spreaders and hook-outs are not standard flyfishing tools, you may not be able to find them at your local fly shop. You can order them from Cabela's, and you can often find them at sporting goods stores or Wal-Mart stores.

I always carry a good pair of needle-nosed pliers with side cutters. Their primary use is for cutting and trimming steel leader. They also work well for pinching down the barb on flies. When I can't locate my hook-outs, pliers work nicely to remove hooks, as long as the pike hasn't taken the fly too deeply.

Polarized sunglasses are an often unheralded "tool" that serves two purposes. First and foremost, they provide safety for your eyes, both from the sun's ultraviolet rays and from flying objects. The latter includes your own large, wind-resistant flies tied on big, sharp hooks, as well as those of other people.

People who fish without eye protection, whatever their method, are asking for trouble. Whenever I see someone fishing without eye protection, I get chills and cringe a bit at the thought of the risk they run. For me, fishing without sunglasses or other eye protection is just not worth the risk of having a hook embedded in my eye or someone else's. Fish smart, fish safe!

Second, polarized sunglasses allow you to see into the fish's world, water clarity permitting. They are the only kind of sunglasses that cut the reflected glare off the surface of the water. I love sight fishing for big pike, and seeing them chase down and eat the fly is a thrill not to

More important than jaw spreaders is another tool not normally associated with fly-fishing—hook-outs.

be missed. Don't go cheap here, since a good pair of polarized sunglasses is an essential and valuable tool.

Proper Handling

This seems the best place to talk a little about how to handle a pike you've caught. I'll risk boring some of you who are experienced with pike and know how to handle them in order to save fish from being mishandled and dying from it. Many times I've seen the thrill and the rush an angler gets from catching a pike on the fly, and too many times, I've seen the same excited angler mishandle the fish or hurriedly rush the fish back into the water without spending time ensuring it has recuperated from the battle. Like trout, pike may have to be cradled for awhile until they're ready to swim away.

The snake grab is the most humane way to handle pike in the water. This can be accomplished by grabbing the pike from above, behind the head where the gill-plate covers end. Be careful not to let your fingers slide into the gill area, since this may harm the pike. If your fingers get too far in, the gill rakers are also quite sharp.

When wade fishing for pike, the snake grab is a highly effective way to handle and control small and medium-sized pike. Larger pike can also be handled in this manner, but you may have to take the fish into shallower water where you will have better control of the situation. A large pike that has been deeply hooked may require the help of your fishing partner for the safety of the fish and yourself.

Small and medium-sized pike may be handled with the snake grab from boats as well. Simply reach over the side of the boat and apply the snake grab while using your free hand to remove the debarbed hook with your hook-outs. This technique is the easiest and safest for angler and pike alike.

When fishing from boats, I never—repeat, never—use regular fishing nets. Nets usually damage the fish's fins and remove the protective slime coating that protects the pike from disease and parasites. I use a cradle instead. A cradle is made from a fine, soft mesh that will not remove the protective slime. Additionally, you don't have to fold the fish to get it in a cradle. Instead it lays flat, allowing the pike to be slid in one end, unhooked, and slid out the other without harm to its fins. Cradles are available from Cabela's or from internet sites.

A large pike that has been deeply hooked may require the help of your fishing partner.

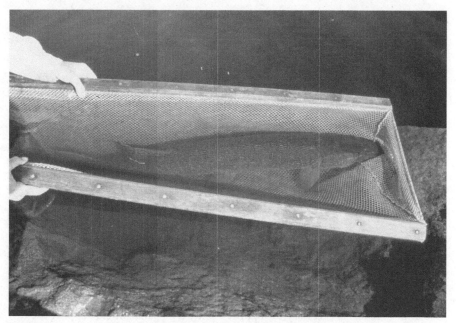

A cradle is made from a fine, soft mesh that will not remove the protective slime.

Unless I'm in need of photographs for a magazine article, I rarely take pike out of the water. It's just not worth the risk to the fish or me. Still I know you may want photographs for your scrapbook. While this is perfectly understandable, take care not to harm the fish and this wonderful, valuable fishery. If you must take a pike out of the water, remember that they're big, long fish. As such, their organs run the length of their body and are extremely vulnerable to damage if the pike is lifted out of the water without its body weight properly supported. Use of both hands is necessary to support a pike. One hand should support the head, while the other supports the body.

In a world where things are constantly being improved, it should really come as no surprise that fishing products continue to get better. Higher modulus graphite, slicker, more durable coatings on fly lines, knotable steel leaders, more creative synthetic fly-tying materials, and breathable Gore-Tex waders and jackets … the fishing world and the technology that goes into the equipment we use every day continues to improve!

Use of both hands is necessary to support a pike. One hand should support the head, while the other supports the body.

EIGHT

PLANNING YOUR NEXT "TRIP OF A LIFETIME"

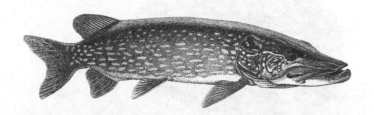

If you fish long enough, you'll eventually want to take a trip of a life-time to some of the more remote and pristine waters in the world to catch your favorite species. I'm not sure who coined the phrase "trip of a lifetime," but whoever did it either didn't travel much or didn't know how to fish! I'm forty-one years old, and I've taken no less than eighty "trips of a lifetime." I plan on taking, at the minimum, eighty more!

Over the years I've been fortunate to fish in some of the most remote and exotic places in the world—Brazil's Amazon jungle for peacock bass, Belize for tarpon, the Bahamas for bonefish, Ascension Bay for permit, and Alaska and Canada for monster pike. I love to travel, see exotic places, and experience the culture of other countries. For me, fishing is a bonus. It's certainly the impetus for my trips, but it's only part of the measure of each trip's success.

I don't always catch the biggest fish nor do I even catch a lot of fish on these trips, but I never walk away disappointed! Why? The answer is quite simple. I take great pride in doing a thorough investigation be-fore settling on a particular lodge or destination, and I always under-stand that fishing is fishing.

Just because you pay thousands of dollars to visit these places doesn't guarantee that you'll catch that "fish of a lifetime." It merely affords you the opportunity to do so. Certainly if you time your trip right, you can have phenomenal fishing and a chance at some truly large pike, but timing requires careful planning and more than a little

Just because you pay thousands of dollars doesn't guarantee that you'll catch that "fish of a lifetime."

luck. Even areas that are known to produce world-class pike do not fish well every day of the year, and the fishing may be off for a week or more. Understanding your goals and keeping your expectations to realistic levels will help make your trip more enjoyable.

In the following section, I'll share the process I use to plan those "trips of a lifetime." I'll tell you how to investigate a destination and give you the right questions to ask to make sure the lodge and lake offer the type of fishing you enjoy most. I cannot urge you strongly enough to take the time to do a thorough inquiry and carefully plan your trip.

Start planning early, take your time, and choose your destination wisely. Don't just settle for a lodge your buddy's friend recommends. The following is my formula for a successful flyfishing adventure. It has served me well on every trip of a lifetime I've taken.

Personal Expectations

From the very beginning, you must establish what it is that you want from a trip. Is it strictly a trophy hunt for big pike? A chance to fish for several species from a luxury lodge? A remote and rustic camp with a lake to yourself? Whatever you're after, you must plan your trip to make sure the lodge or outfitter is capable of providing what you want and to time your trip to give yourself the best opportunity to fulfill your fishing dreams.

Many factors must be considered—timing, accommodations, and more—and I'll cover all of them in this section.

Timing Your Trip

To start the process of planning a trip of a lifetime for pike, let's talk timing. After all, timing *is* everything. Basically, your first decision is whether you want lots of action or the best chance at a true trophy. You should also consider what type of flyfishing—shallow-water or top-water, for example—you enjoy the most and pick the season when it's most productive.

Some people, for instance, want constant action with the occasional trophy-sized fish thrown in. If you fit this category, the post-spawn period is hard to beat. As a general rule, those looking for nothing more than steady action will do well to fish the summer months. Fall is typically more for those seeking quality and size of fish, rather than quantity.

In this section, I'll assume your trip of a lifetime for pike will take you to the North Country, Canada or Alaska. I'll talk about seasonal periods, as opposed to actual months, since the seasons vary greatly from lake to lake. As you move farther north, the seasonal windows become smaller. For example, Nejalini Lake in northern Manitoba offers a very small window, about two to three weeks, for the spectacular post-spawn period, and timing is critical. A week too early and ice on the water will still be a problem. A week too late and the fish start to pull out of the shallows.

Ask the lodge for the average ice-out date and then inquire how long the pike typically hold in the bays before dispersing. Split the difference. If the ice breaks the last week of June and the pike typically hold in the bays until the third week of July, look at the first or second week of July for your target dates. This is the best method to ensure that the ice is off the lake and that the pike will still be stacked in the bays. This is only an example, and every lake is different. Know your questions and ask each lodge the same ones, because their answers will vary greatly.

If the summer cabbage beds are what you want to fish, the lodge should also be able to give you accurate details as to the best times for that. For fall trophies, I recommend hitting the lake just as air and water temperatures begin to cool and the cabbage beds begin to die off. Once again, the lodge, while unable to give you specific dates, will be able to give you a ballpark estimate. You can start looking at dates based on that.

Pre-spawn and Post-spawn

The type of fishing you want to be doing should be an important consideration. You must know the kind of flyfishing you'd enjoy most in order to establish when to go. For shallow-water action, consider the pre-spawn and post-spawn periods.

These are two of the most coveted times of year in flyfishing for pike. Large numbers of fish are gathered in relatively small areas in shallow water. This combination makes for great action, and the ability to sight fish is an added bonus. You'll often be able to pick out individual fish to cast to and watch the action unfold, as pike chase down your flies.

The post-spawn period is also one of the top times for trophies, although it's somewhat of a numbers game, since you have to weed out the small pike to pick up the big fish. If there's a downside to post-spawn pike, it's the fact that the fish are sometimes rather lean from the rigors of the spawn.

Summer and Early Fall

Top-water action is hot during the post-spawn period and the summer months. If you love to fish poppers and divers, this is the time for you. Mid- to late summer is one of my favorite times of year to flyfish for pike in the North, with plenty of fish and lots of action.

Weed beds have had adequate time to mature and grow toward the surface, providing the pike excellent ambush points, but sight-fishing opportunities aren't great, since most of the pike will be parked down in the weeds. Strip your fly alongside the weed beds and watch the pike come charging out, or simply cast your fly into open pockets and watch it disappear in a void of water where a hungry pike is lying in wait.

Fall

If you're truly looking for big fish, the fall period is tough to beat. This is my favorite big-fish time, because the pike have had all summer to fatten up after the spawn. While the post-spawn offers numbers of big fish, the pike typically don't carry a lot of weight. A forty-eight inch pike in the post-spawn may weigh from twenty-five to thirty pounds. That same fish in the fall will weigh anywhere from twenty-eight to thirty-three pounds. Fall pike are definitely fatter and sassier.

So, those of you in pursuit of real trophies should focus your attention on the fall months. As cooler weather starts to settle in during August and September, the weed beds begin to die off, and the big pike really put on the feed bag to fatten up for the winter months and next year's spawn. Water temperatures have begun to cool, allowing big fish access to all parts of the lakes again. The biggest pike I've seen, either in the water or on the end of my line, are those I've seen in fall.

Fall is a time of transition, and pike are on the move. While you're not likely to find numbers of fish concentrated in specific locations, the ones you do come across will probably be some of the biggest pike you'll see all season. For those planning fall trips, I urge you to read again the fall sections covering pike locations in both rivers and lakes and key in to those locations. This is some of the finest fishing to be had, but you'll have to put up with some foul weather and be prepared to cover locations numerous times. Remember—the payoff is BIG!

Accommodations

Now you're ready to form a second set of questions about accommodations and comfort levels. Some of today's most remote lodges are built like a Hilton and are quite capable of running several thousand guests through in a single season. They offer all the amenities, such as saunas, hot tubs, and fully licensed bars! Here is where you should ask yourself some serious questions to separate what you need from what you want. Are you going for the fishing, the comforts, or both?

Some of today's most remote lodges are built like a Hilton.

I've seen some spectacular lodges built on the equivalent of the Dead Sea, and they still sell fishing trips! Personally, I'm willing to compromise on the comfort level for the prospect of better fishing! You probably are, too. There are some lodges that offer both, of course.

At the other end of the spectrum, I've visited many lakes where accommodations were very rustic. The cabin may consist of plywood floors and sides, with a roof that keeps out rain but not mosquitos. These areas receive little pressure, and fishing can be tremendous if you're a pioneer type. The price for a week's stay at these outpost camps is as little as half that charged by the main lodges. You have to decide for yourself whether you have the skill and knowledge to go with some fishing buddies and cook and guide for yourselves! Those who try this without proper knowledge often find themselves in for a very long and disappointing week!

Another consideration related to the lodge or camp you select is wade fishing versus boat fishing. Heavy sediment that builds up in the pike bays of many northern lakes makes wading risky, if not downright dangerous. I've experienced the suck-hole effect of these soft, mucky bottoms firsthand and have spent copious amounts of time trying to get unstuck. At times, I've actually had to grab the boat's gunwales with the outboard running at full throttle to get pulled out.

Use caution and check with the lodge before making plans to wade fish. As you can probably tell, I prefer to fish from a boat much more these days. Becoming a permanent fixture of a northern lake isn't in my plans.

You should now have a rough outline of what your personal expectations are and some general ideas on how to meet them. Now you can shop! Every step of this process is essential. You should be able to tell the lodge as much about yourself as you seek to learn about them! The more information you're willing to dig out, the better prepared you'll be to make decisions about your trip of a lifetime.

Investigating Lodges

Now that you have an idea of what you expect from your trip, you can begin to investigate areas of geographical interest and the lodges that serve them. Before you go to a fishing show and talk to representatives from the lodges, I strongly recommend shopping on the internet. While I don't buy from the internet alone, it's like having a catalog in front of you, with an encyclopedia's worth of information. I always start my pike-destination search online.

From Google or another search engine, simply type in "pike fishing lodges," "pike," or the name of an area or lake you might have in mind. A search like this will bring up anywhere from several hundred to several thousand matches for you to browse through. There's no finer way to begin your research.

It pays to narrow your search by being more specific. For example, when I recently typed in "northern Manitoba lodges," my search netted 8,437 results. By simply adding "fishing" to the search criteria, it cut the number in half. By adding "flyfishing" (or "fly fishing") to the phrase, I reduced the list of sites to about 460.

At this stage, you can browse some sites and do a little window-shopping, but it's time for some serious investigating. You're looking for several criteria when doing your research: the lake's potential to produce trophy pike (more about that later), the quality of equipment, the lodge's familiarity with flyfishing, alternative species available, and the lodge's accommodations. Most lodges offer outpost fishing and daily fly-outs. Those options are worth considering, since conditions may not always be optimal on the main lake.

By the time you visit sites with these things in mind, your list should be down to about twenty lodges that sound most promising. Now you're ready to take your investigation to the next level—phone calls. Many lodges offer a toll-free number; use it! Before calling, compile a list of questions based on your expectations. While your first questions should center around those expectations, there are additional questions you'll want to ask.

Most lodges keep detailed catch rates, and you should ask for them. Some lodges have established a trophy-size limit and only track and count pike that fall into that category, but this still gives you a good base to use for comparison. Catch rates mean little, however, unless you know the number of anglers who fished the lodge during the season.

For example, one lodge bragged about the 1,800 trophy pike of forty inches or better caught during the previous season. The information that they didn't offer and that you won't know unless you ask is that it took 1,200 anglers to catch that many trophy pike. Another lodge

Most lodges offer outpost fishing and daily fly-outs.

counted 997 trophy pike in the previous season, but only had a total of sixty guests fish their waters.

You might think the first lodge has greater trophy potential based on catch-rates alone. A closer examination shows that the second lodge clearly has more to offer. The ratio of trophies to anglers is about 1.5 trophies per angler at the first lodge, compared with 16.6 trophies per angler at the second lodge! While the second lodge is clearly a smaller operation, it has a distinct advantage in the number of trophy pike per guest. Bigger catch-rate numbers by themselves don't always mean better fishing.

Another helpful piece of information that can be pulled from the lodge's logbook is how and when these trophy pike were taken. Most lodge operators make an honest effort to track the manner in which these fish were taken. Conventional anglers will dominate the catches, because they outnumber flyfishers about twenty to one at most lodges. That doesn't matter, because what I want most to know is where in the water column these fish were taken. Were they taken on shallow-running crankbaits or jigged out of deep water?

During certain times of the year, flyfishing is far more productive than fishing with conventional gear. Many lodges have caught on to this fact and are starting to make a strong effort to promote it. They'll be more than happy to share the times of year when flyfishing excels on their waters.

By studying information provided by the lodge's log, you'll also see a pattern of when the biggest fish were caught and how many were caught. This invaluable information can help you focus on a specific time of year when conditions favor both flyfishing and the potential for trophies. If you can get information from several seasons, you can fine tune your timing even more. This step will greatly help you minimize the margin of error in the critical area of timing.

There are other questions worth investigating. Does the lodge have and enforce catch-and-release fishing? While many areas have adopted a strict catch-and-release policy, some lodges still offer the right to kill and take home trophy pike. What a waste! All the northern lakes are incredibly fragile ecosystems that trophy fishing can destroy in a very short time. When this happens, it can take years to replace what has been lost. In the worst-case scenario, the lake and the pike never recover!

Imagine spending thousands of dollars and traveling halfway across North America only to catch stunted pike just like you can catch in your local lake. In addition to inquiring about catch-and-release, you should ask how long the lodge has promoted their catch-and-release policy. I always look long and hard at lakes where the policy has recently been put into effect, because severe damage may have occurred prior to its implementation.

Another often-overlooked question that should be asked is how many lodges are on the lake you'll be fishing. In some cases, other lodges may use the lake as their fly-out option! Most of these destination lodges are nestled on expansive lakes that have literally hundreds of miles of shoreline. These larger lakes can handle more than one lodge without too much turmoil.

Nothing burns my craw more than going out on the water and seeing anglers from other lodges. It kind of spoils one of my expectations— solitude. Or, at least, sole fishing rights. So if there is more than one lodge located on the lake you're considering, always check to see if it ever becomes an issue. Consider the overall size of the lake and the distance between the lodges before letting the answers affect your decision.

Another consideration is the make-up of the lake, including the bottom characteristics and vegetation. Bottom characteristics can be a very important factor if you wish to wade fish. As I mentioned earlier, many of these lakes are quite "old," and over time a great deal of sediment has built up in them, making wade fishing questionable. What appears to be an easily waded bottom may actually be a giant suck hole from which you'll never be able to free yourself. Use caution and heed the lodge's advice to avoid getting yourself in, shall we say, a sticky situation.

Find out what other species are available and when they're available. In Alaska, alternate species include sheefish and salmon, while many of the Canadian lakes have walleye, lake trout, and grayling in addition to pike. Having alternatives to fall back on may help save a trip when conditions are less than favorable for pike. Cold, miserable, rainy days might not be conducive to great pike flyfishing, but walleye fishing can be outstanding. And the answer to your question is, yes! Walleye can be caught on a fly, and I've had some terrific days catching them.

In Alaska, alternative species include sheefish and salmon.

Walleye can be caught on a fly, and I've had some terrific days catching them.

Ask if the lake has ever been commercially fished. Most people are puzzled by this idea, since they don't realize that many of these lakes have, at one time or another, been harvested for the market. In rare cases, some lakes have been over-harvested, and one or more species have been depleted, throwing the whole fishery out of whack. In these cases, the forage base is also affected, making the fishery unstable and unpredictable. Again, this is rare, but worth asking about.

How long is the season? Many of the lodges work on a short season, sometimes only from June through August. If you want to fish the late-fall period and split your time between pike and pre-spawn lakers, such a lodge isn't a great option. It will have shut down prior to the first hard freeze, which typically prompts the movement of lake trout to their shallow spawning grounds and initiates the pike's last heavy feeding before the lake freezes.

Ask each lodge what their prime times are. Just because you experienced good fishing in southern Manitoba last June, don't assume you'll find the same conditions a hundred miles to the north at the same time. Again, timing is critical, and the pike's seasonal movements vary considerably from one piece of water to the next and sometimes within the same lake. I've been on large Canadian lakes where pike in the southern end of the lake were in the post-spawn period while pike on the north end were in pre-spawn and spawn!

You should inquire if a representative of the lodge will be visiting your area for a fishing show. This will allow you to meet with the operators and their guides and can be invaluable. For one thing, it allows you to put a face with a name and establishes a comfort level between yourself and the lodge you're considering.

If you're still interested in a lodge after listening to the sales pitch and the answers to your questions, there's still one more thing you should do. Remember, like any good accountant, lodge owners can still make the numbers look any way they want them to look, and they have to be good salesmen. So, you should also ask for a list of guest references, and then it's time to get back on the phone.

Take the time, spend a few dollars, and call some of the people who've fished at the lodge. Ask what time of year they fished, inquire about what type of fishing they were doing, see how many times they've visited the lodge, and ask them any question that you asked the lodge itself. These people aren't paid by the lodge. They simply had good experiences they don't mind sharing.

By the time you've finished this process, you should have narrowed your search down to two or three choices! It's time to call these lodges and inquire about promotional videos showing the lodge, the fishing, and the guides at work. You could request this information earlier in the process, but what are you going to do with several hundred promotional videos and brochures? I refuse promotional information when it's offered, until I get down to the few lodges that have made the cut. For me, too much information like that and everything starts to run together.

Now you should have the foundation to make knowledgeable decisions about where to go, when to go, and what to expect once you get there. There are still several items we need to discuss—costs, weather, travel, and what to bring.

Costs

So, how much should you expect to spend? Depending on the length of stay, what plan you choose, and what lodge you pick, prices will range from $2,000 to as much as $3,500 per week, on average. There are, of course, cheaper and more expensive trips, and as with most things, you get what you pay for. Cheaper rates may require a trip during the off-season, when fishing is less than ideal. However, more expensive trips don't necessarily mean better fishing. The higher cost is usually due to the degree of luxury and the amenities available at a remote destination.

For those on a budget who are confident of their ability to locate and catch pike on new bodies of water, outpost camps offer a less expensive option. These camps are set up on remote parts of the lake or on separate lakes by themselves. They often offer solitude and pristine fishing for the adventurous angler at a fraction of the price of a stay at a lodge. These do-it-yourself camps should be thoroughly investigated before you go, by checking the same information that you would for any other lodge. Seven days on a lake that only offers small to medium-sized fish or inadequate numbers of fish can make for a long week of cheap fishing!

My suggestion is to not cut too many corners, while still trying to be frugal and get the biggest bang for your buck. I've found that most moderately priced lodges offer all I need in the way of modern comforts. As long as the fishing is good, then the world is right by me. Your personal needs will dictate whether you need to stay at the "Hilton" in the middle of nowhere or if a log cabin with adequate accommodations fits the bill. By the way, most of the high-priced lodges are the same ones pushing thousands of people through the doors each season. They're often more concerned with the almighty dollar than with providing fishing that is above the norm.

One other consideration that comes into play in the cost equation is the length of your stay. Most lodges offer three-, four-, and seven-day trips. The price varies accordingly, with a three-day trip costing around $1,500 and a seven-day trip averaging around $2,800. I must urge you to use caution with three-day trips, particularly during the early part of the season, because you may have cold, rainy weather every day. A seven-day trip will probably assure you of several days

As long as the fishing is good, then the world is right.

of decent weather. For me, a shorter trip isn't worth the risk of hitting bad conditions, and when you factor in transportation costs and time, it isn't much of a bargain, either.

Finally, I understand the need for lodges to make money. After all, that's why they're in business. But there are lodges that put equal value on maintaining a stable fishery. They understand these fragile systems can only handle so much pressure. These lodges have struck a balance between the two, and they are the lodges I seek out and gladly spend my money on.

Tipping

Tipping is an additional cost you should consider as part of the total you'll spend on the trip. While there are no rules that state you must tip your guide or the lodge staff, it's expected, and if they treat you right, they should be tipped accordingly. Many lodges pay their staffs well, but they also assume that they'll be tipped.

If your guide shows you a good time and does his or her utmost to keep you on fish during your stay, you should show your appreciation at the end of your visit. Typically there are two anglers per boat and guide, and the average tip is in the range of $50 to $100 per day per boat, split between the two anglers. Again, this is only a guideline. You and your fishing partner for the week will make the final decision.

It's also customary to tip the lodge staff if their service merits it. You'll be served breakfast and dinner from the time you arrive to the time you leave. These people work very hard and deserve to be recognized. There are also staff members who take care of your cabin and make sure you have clean towels on a daily basis. There may also be a laundry service at your camp. Due to the large number of people involved, the tip money is usually pooled and split at the end of the week. The guideline here is to plan on $75 to $150 per week for your contribution, depending on the service provided and what you can afford.

Travel Considerations

I shy away from lodges that can be reached by automobile. These lodges can offer excellent fishing, but the lakes often face high pressure as a result of the easy access. While offering distinct advantages, more remote locations can be difficult to reach. True fly-in lodges are so remote they can only be accessed by plane.

On a seven-day trip, you might actually be looking at a total time of nine days or more. At a minimum, an overnight stay on the way to the lodge is usually required. On a typical Tuesday-to-Tuesday, seven-day trip to Manitoba, for example, you can expect to arrive in Winnipeg on Monday and stay overnight before catching your charter to the lodge the following morning. On your return trip, you may be able to hit connecting flights and make it all the way home in one day's time, barring weather delays. In other words, you could theoretically leave the lodge Tuesday morning and be home for dinner Tuesday night.

This only an example, so be sure to work out carefully all parts of your itinerary to and from the lodge. As a courtesy, most lodges work with travel agencies that help ease this part of the planning and ensure you arrive where you're supposed to be, when you're supposed to be there.

Last, but not least, when it comes to traveling to some of these remote regions, keep in mind that you will travel in smaller aircraft. My trip to Alaska each year requires three flights before I reach the lodge. I typically fly a 767 to Anchorage. From Anchorage, I fly in a twenty-passenger Metropolitan turboprop to the small town of Aniak. There I transfer to a six-passenger Helio-Courier float plane for the final leg of the journey.

Each plane gets decidedly smaller as you travel into more remote areas. I bring this up to make two important points. First, if you're prone to airsickness, bring appropriate medicine to help ease the nausea and make the travel portion of your trip more enjoyable for yourself and for the people you'll be fishing with for a week. Second, pack accordingly. Most lodges have weight restrictions for a reason. The small planes simply can't carry the passengers and all the gear they might want to bring. Weight becomes an issue when you pack everything you're afraid you might need. I want to be the first to warn you, here and now—don't overload your gear. If you do, you may be forced to leave some of it behind and then hope like hell it's where you left it when you return.

Each plane gets decidedly smaller as you travel into more remote areas.

If you're crossing the U.S. border, you'll need to be aware of customs regulations. You can check the current regulations and traveler's advisories on the internet. As you know, security is at a heightened level now and regulations may change at any time.

While entry into Canada can be made with a valid driver's license and a birth certificate, I strongly urge you to get a passport to make clearing customs easier. Acquiring a passport is pretty painless but can take upwards of six months. Passports are good for ten years. If you're really serious about traveling to fish, you'll want one anyway.

To obtain a passport, I suggest you visit the U. S. State Department's internet site. Here you'll find all the necessary information to apply for a passport and links to download the application form.

Weather Considerations

When you visit the North Country, you can expect to face an array of weather conditions, from snow in the spring and fall to thunderstorms during the brief summer months. Of course, the farther north you go, the shorter the season of warm weather. If weather is a consideration for you when you go fishing, understanding what to expect is vital.

At most northern lodges, the open-water season is from June to September. June highs average between sixty-five and seventy-five degrees with lows in the thirty- to forty-degree range. On a typical seven-day trip, you can expect a day or two of cold, damp weather. In July, warm, stable weather is the norm, with average daytime highs of seventy-five to eighty-five degrees and nighttime lows a comfortable forty to fifty degrees.

August is the swing month, where the short summer quickly gives way to the onset of fall. Wild weather swings occur, and mild, warm weather can quickly change to cold, rainy days. Be prepared to deal with eighty-degree heat one day and forty degrees with driving rains the next. This is trophy time for pike, but being prepared to deal with all types of weather is a must. By the time September rolls around, fall is in full swing. Days are quite cool, but pleasant, and nighttime temperatures drop below the freezing mark on a regular basis. The first snows of the season will not be far behind.

The bottom line is that weather in the Far North is unpredictable at best. From snow in June to bone-chilling rains in August, no matter when you plan your trip, learn to expect and deal with the unexpected. With the weight restrictions on baggage, what to take in the way of clothing and rain gear, not to mention tackle, will begin to fill your thoughts as your trip draws near.

What to Bring

As you now know, many factors must be considered when packing for your trip. The weight restrictions for baggage I've already mentioned apply on most flights to lodges and outpost camps. Your lodge will advise you about these restrictions, and a dry run at home to pack and weigh your gear is a good idea. That way, if your luggage is overweight, you can decide at home, not at a distant airport, what to leave behind.

It's tough to know what to take on any trip, but a trip up north demands extra care, especially in the clothing you take. Ill-prepared anglers do not have a good time. My experience in selecting clothing and appropriate tackle should help.

Clothing

Your clothing needs will obviously be based on the time of year you're going, but as you've seen, the weather can change drastically in the North Country, regardless of the time of year. I suggest you plan to dress in layers, so you can add or take off clothing depending on the weather. Quality clothing—especially rain gear—is often overlooked, but you shouldn't go cheap. Long, cold, wet boat rides can be a chilling experience if you're not prepared.

My layers of clothing starts with insulated underwear and heavy wool socks. Next I add a mock turtleneck and a long-sleeved wind shirt. For pants, I wear blue jeans. I carry two jackets. The first is my personal favorite, a Simms Windstopper Jacket, made with microfleece. It's warm and lightweight enough that I don't feel like I'm tied up in it, and it's very comfortable when I'm casting.

My second coat is a Simms Guide Jacket. This Gore-Tex coat provides outstanding water resistance during inclement weather, and it makes an excellent shell to throw over my first coat for the long, cool boat rides. I also pack a pair of Simms Gore-Tex rain pants that I keep

Quality clothing—especially rain gear—is often overlooked, but you shouldn't go cheap.

in my boat bag for rainy days. While Simms is my personal preference for these items, there are many other fine manufacturers offering similar products that work equally well.

With the fickle weather, I also pack a good pair of waterproof boots. I prefer to wear my old fishing sneakers when I can, but when the weather turns cold and damp, the boots come in handy. While I prefer to wear a baseball cap, I also have a wool stocking cap for the boat rides. A good pair of wool gloves will also serve you well during those long rides and on cold, rainy days.

One last clothing accessory to consider is a good pair of Gore-Tex waders if wade fishing is an option. Many lodges now keep waders on hand that can be borrowed. This can save a lot of space in your baggage and some weight, as well. Most lodges also offer daily laundry service—something else you should check for—which minimizes the changes of clothes you have to take and saves more space and weight.

Other accessory items that are a must include a good pair of high-quality, polarized sunglasses (I always pack a back-up pair), sunscreen, and insect repellent. Don't forget the insect repellent!

Tackle and Flies

In this section, I'll describe the tackle I typically take on my trips to Canada. Your preferences may dictate different rod sizes and other tackle options. The lake you're visiting may also influence your choices, based on the other species of fish available.

For pike fishing, I take at least two nine-weight rods, in case one gets broken. I also pack a five-weight rod if grayling or walleye are available. My nine-weight doubles as a rod for lake trout, sheefish, and salmon. My pike reels consist of two Ross Reels Big Game 4s, one rigged with a floating pike line, and the other with a seven-foot sink tip. I also carry a spare spool rigged with a full-sink line. My grayling and walleye setup also includes two reels, again rigged with a floating line and a sink-tip line.

By now you know I like to tie my own leaders. I carry, at all times, no less than five twenty-five-yard spools of sixteen-pound Mason hard monofilament and an equal amount of twenty-pound, nylon-coated steel leader. This gives me more than enough leader material for a week of steady pike action. For lake trout, I use the same leaders, because lake trout have a very raspy set of teeth. For grayling, I use tapered 4X leaders. A half-dozen or so of these leaders will do for your evening grayling fishing. For walleye I carry 0X leaders. Under normal circumstances, I rarely fish for anything other than pike on these trips, unless the pike aren't cooperating.

Remember, this is my Canadian gear. If I were going to Alaska, my secondary gear would be trout and salmon oriented.

Last—but not certainly least—my fly selection for a week of pike fishing includes three to four dozen pike streamers and a dozen or so top-water flies. The lodge will help you in selecting the best patterns and colors. I also carry a couple of dozen nymphs and streamers for grayling and a dozen or so Clouser Minnows for walleye.

Remember to pack your pike tools. While most lodges provide guides with the tools necessary to handle a pike's dental requirements, I still prefer to carry my own. I always bring a set of jaw spreaders, oversized hook-outs, and a good pair of needle-nosed pliers with side cutters for cutting steel leaders.

Miscellaneous tackle includes reel lube, fly-line cleaner, a thermometer, and a hook sharpener or file. Don't forget you'll need a waterproof bag to carry your gear on the boat.

Your bags are packed and you're ready to go fishing, right? Just to be sure, take a look at the following checklist of the things I pack. Modify it to suit your needs and use it to be sure you don't forget anything. The nearest shopping center will be a long way away.

Travel Checklist

I've traveled all over the world to some of the finest flyfishing locations, but I still don't trust my memory when it comes to packing. So, I've put together a checklist for each species and location to make it less likely I'll arrive at a remote destination lacking something I'll need to make the trip successful.

The following is my basic northern pike checklist for fishing in Alaska and Canada. I've given the details of my tackle choices, such as the kinds and numbers of rods, in the section on tackle, but you should specify them on the checklist you develop for your own needs.

____ Passport
____ Passport copy (kept in a separate location)
____ Airline tickets
____ Trip itinerary
____ Cash and travelers' checks
____ Emergency phone numbers
____ Toiletry bag (including medications)

____ Pike fly rods
____ Fly rods for other species
____ Pike fly reels
____ Fly reels for other species
____ Spare spools
____ Reel lube
____ Spare fly lines
____ Fly line cleaner
____ Pike flies
____ Flies for other species
____ Pike leaders
____ Leaders for other species
____ Hook-outs
____ Jaw spreaders
____ Pliers with side-cutters
____ Hook sharpener or file
____ Boat bag (waterproof)
____ Sunglasses (plus a back-up pair)
____ Thermometer

____ Waders
____ Wading shoes
____ Rain jacket
____ Wind jacket
____ Rain pants
____ Long-sleeved shirts
____ T-shirts
____ Mock turtlenecks

_____ Jeans

_____ Casual pants (for dinner at the lodge)

_____ Thermal underwear (tops and bottoms)

_____ Underwear

_____ Socks

_____ Baseball cap

_____ Stocking cap

_____ Gloves

_____ Camera/film/batteries

_____ First-aid kit

_____ Sunscreen

_____ Insect repellent

Overview

Most lodges are built on lakes known for their world-class fishing, but that's not necessarily the case. Even when it is, without proper planning, you may not be on the lake at the right time for the kind of fly-fishing experience you want.

By taking the time to prepare and investigate your trip properly, you can make sure the lodge not only offers, but can produce what you're looking for from your trip of a lifetime. Every bit of information you search out will take you one step closer to reaching pike fishing's holy grail and the ultimate reward of being in the right place at the right time.

INDEX

BARRY REYNOLDS has co-authored three previous books—*Pike on the Fly*, *Beyond Trout*, and *Carp on the Fly*. He has written for *Fly Rod and Reel*, *American Angler*, *Warmwater Fly Fishing*, *Wild on the Fly*, and *Fly-Tyer Magazine*. He has made guest appearances on *ESPN Outdoors*, *Fly Fishing America*, and other television shows. He is featured in a video on flyfishing for pike. Barry is the current world record holder in the I.G.F.A. twelve-pound-tippet line class with a northern pike weighing thirty-three pounds, eight ounces. He has caught eleven pike over fifty inches, with a personal best pike weighing thirty-five pounds, eight ounces. He lives in Aurora, Colorado, with his wife Susan, and their children, Christie and Michael.